Virginia Driving Hawk Sneve

VIRGINIA DRIVING HAWK SNEVE

COMPLETING

THE CIRCLE

UNIVERSITY OF NEBRASKA PRESS: LINCOLN AND LONDON

⊛The paper in this book meets the minimum requirements of American National
Standard for Information Sciences—Permanence of Paper for Printed Library
Materials, ANSI Z39.48-1984.

First Bison Books printing: 1998

Library of Congress Cataloging in Publication Data

Sneve, Virginia Driving Hawk.
Completing the circle / Virginia Driving Hawk Sneve.
p. cm.
Includes bibliographical references.
ISBN 0-8032-4226-3 (alk. paper)
ISBN 0-8032-9254-6 (pa: alk. paper)
1. Dakota women—Biography.   2. Dakota women—History.
3. Dakota Indians—Social life and customs.   I. Title.
E99.D1S6276   1995
973'.04975—dc20
94-22777   CIP

For my granddaughters

CONTENTS

ILLUSTRATIONS

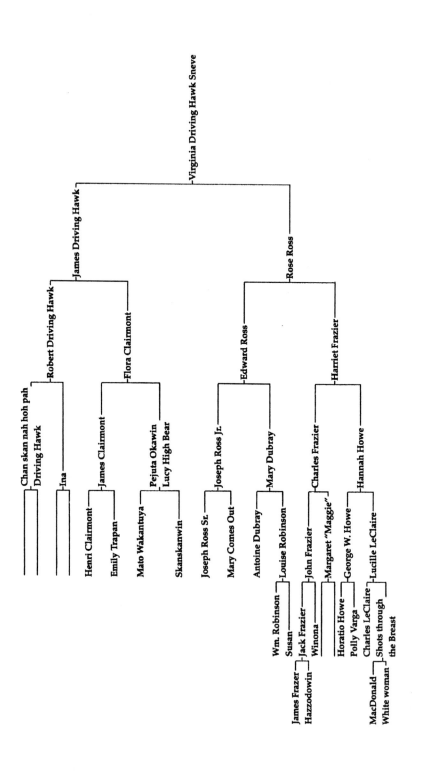

INTRODUCTION

There is a star quilt on the bed in my home. The once bright tones of red, lavender, blue, and brown are now soft pastel hues blended into an eight-pointed star. It was a wedding gift from my grandmother, Flora Driving Hawk, and each time I make the bed I remember how she stitched the diamond pieces together. I think of how she and her women friends sat around the quilt frame, gossiping, laughing, sighing as they stitched the joys and sorrows of their lives into the quilt. Later, after she died, I learned to quilt, honoring her request to finish the star quilt tops she had made for each of my three children.

As I fashion a quilt, it reminds me of life formed about a youthful core of pulsing hopes and bright dreams that broaden to multihued circles of womanhood. The circle widens until the blended hues narrow to a single-colored point of the star that is life's end.

Just as the diamond pieces are joined, so is my life bound to the lives of my mother and grandmothers. I knew some of the pieces of their lives, yet I yearned to know more to join them into a whole. My mother and her sisters had pieces of what I looked for—pictures in albums, envelopes, and shoeboxes waiting for the day when there would be time to organize, identify, and share them with relatives. On a 1988 Christmas in California, Mother, Rose Ross Posey, my daughter Shirley Kay Sneve, and I decided to put together a picture book of our relatives.

After selecting photos, we realized that a brief family history would have to accompany the pictures. I wanted the chronicle to be as accurate as possible, so I spent several years researching records and published and unpublished histories and interviewing relatives.

As I gathered pieces of information from within the family circle, I found that there were still gaps when it came to the grandmothers.

To the Dakotas and Lakotas (Sioux) and other American Indians, the circle is a sacred symbol of all life. A great deal is known of that circle, yet, just as within my family's circle, there are great gaps because so little is known about the women. I had first realized this when researching a paper, "The Women of the Circle," for a presentation at the Nordland Fest at Augustana College in Sioux Falls, South Dakota, in 1985. Now, as I began a personal search for my relatives, this great lack of knowledge made me feel incomplete.

The grandmothers I knew as a child were caring, loving women who made me feel warmly secure, and I took their love for granted. As an adult, I came to appreciate these wise, dignified, modest women who were teachers and healers, devoutly religious. They were honest, hardworking women, virtuous helpmates to their husbands, and they considered children a blessing. They raised their children with Christian moral strictness, yet instilled respect for their cultural heritage. Their role was patterned after that of their prereservation mothers and grandmothers: to be a mate, companion, and homemaker to a husband and to bear and raise his children.

They called themselves *Sioux*, not knowing the Ojibwa and French origin of the name, and out of respect for them I use this as a generic term, clarifying band or location with *Dakota* or *Lakota*.

Dakota means "friends" or "an alliance of friends," and the tribe was an alliance of three major divisions—the Santee or eastern Sioux, the Teton or western Sioux, and the Yankton Sioux—each of which was further divided into subgroups. For example, the Teton Sioux comprised seven bands: the Sicangu (or Brulé), Oglala, Hunkpapa, Minneconjou, Sihasapa (or Blackfeet), Oohenumpa (or Two Kettles), and Itazipco (or Sans Arcs).

In historical times before the U.S. government forced them onto reservations, the Santees inhabited the wooded lakeshores and riverbanks of the upper Mississippi River region, the Tetons ranged across the northern plains from the Missouri River to the Rockies, and the Yanktons occupied the territory between the other two groups. They all spoke essentially the same language, one that is still very much alive today, although their dialects differ slightly. The Santees speak Dakota and the Yanktons Nakota, whereas the Teton dialect is known as Lakota, a name by which the people often refer to themselves.

My Sioux heritage is from all three groups, blended with Ponca,

French, Scots, and English. I wanted to know how this came to be and whether this heterogeneity of races and cultures and this polyglot mingling had affected my life and my writing.

My grandmothers—and all Indian grandmothers—were better than mothers because, whereas an Indian woman's first duty was to see to the needs of her husband, grandmothers saw to the needs of their grandchildren. Before the imposition of formal education, they were teachers instructing through stories that had examples of proper behavior or were history lessons of tribe and family. I was fortunate in receiving this instruction and in remembering the lessons.

In my quest I began with those oral histories: legends, facts, and family stories that were a mixture of legend and fact, but all gleaned from the telling to which I had listened avidly as a child. As I reviewed them, I remembered that grade school through college history classes either ignored Indians or presented them as bloodthirsty savages or nature's noble pagans. There was no place for either in the nation's Manifest Destiny. I wondered whether my family stories were wrong—"bad" because they didn't fit what I was taught. Luckily, Dr. Parker, one of my undergraduate history professors, encouraged me to explore my family's oral history because such a source was indeed credible and valid.

Keeping this information passed down orally in mind, I next went to written sources to supplement what I had heard, to place the oral history within the context of the written. What little I found as I explored the written histories of the time periods in which my grandmothers had lived, seeking knowledge of what it was to be an Indian woman in another era, came from anthropological studies and histories written from a male perspective.

In going to written records, I consulted Episcopal and Roman Catholic archives and U.S. census reports. I am grateful to the Rapid City Public Library, the Leland Case Library at Black Hills State University in Spearfish, the Rapid City Central High School Indian Studies Library, the Center for Western Studies in Sioux Falls, and the St. Francis Indian Mission, St. Francis, South Dakota, for their invaluable assistance in this quest.

I searched published histories of the eastern Sioux tribes, the Santees, who were the first encountered by Europeans in what is now Michigan, Wisconsin, Minnesota, and Canada. Their reports furnished the basis for the history of the Indians in Minnesota written by the Reverend Edward Duffield Neill in the 1850s. George W. Kingsbury, Dakota Territory historian, relied on Neill in his 1915 history of the Dakotas, or Sioux, in Dakota Territory, and I, too, have relied on him in telling of the eastern Sioux.

Doane Robinson's 1904 *History of the Dakota or Sioux Indians*, written when he was secretary of the South Dakota Department of History, extensively quoted or used Neill's work. Although Robinson's account is the first significant attempt to chronicle Sioux history, it deals largely with the Santee and Yankton groups and only meagerly with the western Tetons, who played a prominent role in South Dakota. But that is not unusual. In any written history of the western tribes, there are no detailed accounts like those found in Neill's work because the Tetons were not concentrated in one location as were the eastern Sioux, whom French voyageurs encountered on the waterways. After acquiring horses, the nomadic Tetons roamed from the Missouri to the Rockies and from Canada to the central plains. Little wonder that there are contradictory spellings of names and different names for the same person encountered by white men in various areas of the country.

Doane Robinson's history, as noted by Jack Marken and Herbert Hoover in their *Bibliography of the Sioux* (1980), "reflected the nineteenth century anti-Indian bias, and included little Indian viewpoint even though Robinson was in continuous contact with Sioux people" (118). Unfortunately, this is also true of Doane Robinson's other works about the Sioux of South Dakota and typical of historians of Robinson's era.

These male historians used male sources (missionaries, military men, and fur traders) in narrating their Sioux histories, and those sources reported few events involving the women of the tribes, rarely even noting their names. Women of any race were generally ignored in written histories of the United States. Indian women were noted only if they were "princesses" like Pocohontas or "noble savages" like Sacagawea who in some way or other aided white men.

In the nineteenth century female writers such as Helen Hunt Jackson and Flora Warren Seymour wrote of American Indians, but, because they were of a generation for whom women were still second-class citizens, their narratives reflect this view. Jackson's sympathetically written *Ramona* is filled with nineteenth-century sentimental bias, even though her *Century of Dishonor* is now considered, in the words of Marken and Hoover, "a classic indictment against federal Indian policy" (1980, 107).

Two early twentieth-century Sioux writers, Charles Eastman, a Santee, and Gertrude Bonnin (Zitkala-Sâ), a Yankton, produced autobiographical works that included some details of Indian women, but again in the sentimental style popular with that era's readers of Indian stories. Eastman's wife, Elaine Goodale Eastman, left more in terms of both quantity and quality in her writings of the western Sioux's early reservation experience than any other chronicler of that time. She also revealed valuable information about the lives of Sioux women during the early reservation period.

Bonnin's stories can be categorized as "good" and "bad" Indian stories. The "good" stories include tales of a free child of nature based on her own life and tales of brave and courageous Indians based on legend. Like Charles Eastman's retelling of Dakota legends, Bonnin's *Old Indian Legends* was well received by non-Indians and often used in schools. These "good Indian" stories were readily published in eastern publications, favorably reviewed, and critically acclaimed.

The "bad Indian" stories, fiction based on the actual life of early reservation Indians, were received negatively by reviewers, who made no comment on the literary merit of the writing. These stories told about Indian life the way it was: the disintegration of the traditions and values and the extreme poverty and destitution of reservation life. I too encountered such stories of Indian life in my family's history.

I found Bonnin's "good" and "bad" Indian stories important because, whereas Charles Eastman reported the way life had been earlier for the Dakotas, Bonnin was the first Sioux to write truthfully as an Indian about the traumatic effects of cultural disintegration. I empathized with Bonnin and the ambivalence of a mixed-blood, female author trying to walk in two worlds. Both she and Charles Eastman described the values and customs of the Dakotas, but Bonnin and Elaine Goodale Eastman showed that these values were still treasured in early reservation life.

Another Sioux scholar and author important to my work is Ella Deloria, who contributed to the anthropological and linguistic knowledge of the western tribes. Although her posthumously published *Waterlily* (1988b) is a novel, it is also an authentic account based on the author's scholarly studies and the oral history of her people. It was helpful in substantiating what my grandmothers had related.

My grandmothers lived during the time these authors and historians wrote, but they did not write their stories—they told them to their grandchildren. Some of what they said can be found in written sources; some of it is only in the memory of the people.

My thanks go to my mother, Rose Ross Posey, Aunt "Dolly" Mary Hannah Ross LaPointe, and Great-aunt Estelle Frazier Recountre for their help in gathering pictures, anecdotes, facts, and dates. As I tapped their memories, I realized that my own memories of their fathers, my grandfathers, were limited. I regret this now but understand the reason: young girls spent most of their time with other females, and women lived longer than men.

However, the men of my family contributed invaluably to my search, especially my father, James Driving Hawk, who kept a diary as part of his duties as a priest of the Episcopal Church. His terse entries triggered recollections in my mind. I'm also grateful to my uncle Donald Ross, who wrote down what his mother, Harriet, had said, and shared it with me. A priceless source was the journal of the Reverend Charles Frazier, memoirs written by my great-grandfather of his years as a Congregational missionary. Originally written in Dakota, the journal was translated and edited by one of Charles's grandsons, my cousin Art Raymond. Another cousin, Jim Bill Ross, searching to document the degree of Indian blood of his children, gathered tons of Bureau of Indian Affairs data, which he shared with me.

There are still pieces missing, but this assistance from within the family helped fill in the gaps so that I've learned more of who my grandmothers were, where they lived, and what their lives were like.

The story of my grandmothers and other women of the circle is found in a gleaning of both oral and written sources and is the thread that stitched the pieces of knowledge into a beautiful star quilt.

In just about every Sioux family there is a woman who is honored for her beautifully crafted star quilts. Each quilt is different even though the design is similar to every other, just as each woman has her own family history, her own quest. I hope that this account of my search will encourage other Native American women to search out and take pride in the pattern of their heritage.

COMPLETING THE CIRCLE

UNCI

Unci, grandma seated on the Rosebud plain,
tossed sage, smothering supper's flame
to acrid smudge meeting the stars,
stinging our drowsy eyes, it drove away
mosquitoes.
Unci told evening stories
weaving Lakota into English.
Words painting pictures on eager minds,
hands counterpoint
to Iktomi's tricks, turtle's wisdom.
We laughed as we learned.
                          from "Story Tellers"

Unci was Flora Clairmont Driving Hawk, wife to Robert, mother of six; she was my paternal grandmother and a storyteller who stirred my childish imagination, which inspired my adult mind to tell stories. Flora told stories in the evenings during the several summers my brother and I stayed with our Driving Hawk grandparents.

She was a short woman, but I never thought her small because of the size of her spirit. *Strong willed* and *determined* are the adjectives that come to mind, certainly not *assertive* as a feminist because she was first a wife and mother. She was determined that her children and grandchildren be independent, educated, and Christian. She was strong willed in achieving what she considered to be the best way and would not tolerate disobedience to her instructions.

My hair began to gray when I was in my thirties, while hers, at eighty, was still black. I shampooed it for her and envied the color, but was saddened at how wispy thin it had become. I remember on one of those summer evenings of my childhood she let me brush her hair, and its glossy thickness reached to the middle of her back. I thought it was beautiful, but she wouldn't wear it loose to shawl over her shoulders, instead plaiting it into a single braid that she coiled and pinned at the nape of her neck.

Her head was round under the smooth coif, and so were her black eyes, but they could narrow to angry slits when she was displeased. This wasn't often, for we, her only grandchildren, were cherished and probably spoiled. Most of the time she hummed the tune of "Yusa meye, yea Jejovah," her favorite from the Lakota Episcopal hymnal. Sometimes she whistled it as she went about her chores.

The day's heat lingered in Flora's small house, so she often cooked supper on an open fire in the yard. After the meal, we stayed outdoors until the evening breeze cooled the house. After I helped wash the dishes with water heated over the fire, I ran to play with my brother while Grandma and Grandpa sat on kitchen chairs near the house until the sun set and we had to come home. It was still too hot to go to bed, so Grandpa would throw a handful of sage on the fire's dying embers. The bitter smoke made my eyes water, but it drove away the mosquitoes. I would lie on the ground watching the sparks fly up to meet the stars in the darkening prairie sky and listen to Grandma tell a story.

So vivid is this memory that thirty years later it was easy to relive those evenings, and its setting became part of the stories I wrote for children. I could not replicate in written English Flora's manner or voice, but her natural technique influenced my style.

Flora used her voice well in her narrations. It never varied much in pitch or tone but ranged in volume from a near whisper to a shout. In the wavering firelight, her gestures enhanced the telling. Her head bobbed, shook, or nodded; she pursed her lips to indicate "over there"; her hands beckoned, waved, followed the lightning's zigzag and echoed the clap of thunder, or became the beat of a drum; she sat tall, proudly or in anger, or she slumped in despair. She stirred my imagination, or perhaps it was already so charged that I imagined it all.

They say [Flora's stories always began] that somewhere over by the Pipestone Quarries [in present-day Minnesota], the people gathered to pray to Wakantanka. Two young men were sent out to hunt. They walked along—they didn't have horses yet—until there was bright light, or something, in front of them so that they had to stop. Their eyes got used to the bright light; they saw a beautiful girl all dressed in white.

"I am from the Buffalo People," she said. "They sent me to talk to your people. I want you to go tell them that I will come to see them." She was so pretty that one of the young men didn't pay attention to what she was saying.

"Tell your people to have a council tepee ready for me." She told them how to set it up.

The young man who thought she was so pretty was not listening because he had bad thoughts about her. He tried to grab her. "Don't!" the other young man yelled, but it was too late. There was a crash of thunder, and a big cloud came over the bad man and the pretty girl. When it cleared away, the bad man was a skeleton on the ground. Ever after the White Buffalo Calf Woman protects girls from bad men.

The other young man was afraid, but the woman told him that because he did not have bad thoughts, he would be all right. So he went back to his village and told the people all that had happened and what the woman told them to do.

The people were all excited. They got everything ready. Then she came, walking from the east with the sunrise, all dressed in white and so beautiful. In her hands she carried a bundle with a pipe in it. She walked to the tepee. Its door opened to the east (which is why tepees are always set up that way). She walked in and turned to the left (which is why that is the woman's side). She sat down with her legs placed to her right side and tucked her feet in (which is why women sit that way). When she talked, everyone understood her, but the women noticed that some of the words she used were different from the way the men spoke (which is why women have a special way of talking).

She told the people about Wakantanka. She said that she was the people's sister and that she had brought them a sacred pipe. The pipe was for peace, not for war.

She talked to the women. "My sisters," she called them, "you have hard things to do in your life. You have pain when you have babies, and it's hard to raise children. But you are important, because without you there would be no people. So you will have babies for your husband. You will feed your man and children; you will make their clothes; you will make the tepees. You will be good wives."

Then she spoke to the girls who weren't married. "You will be pure until you get married. When you do get married, you will always be faithful to your man."

Then she talked to the men. "My brothers," she called them, "you must have good thoughts about girls so that they will be pure when they get married. When you take wives, you will be kind to all of them" (because she said 'wives,' the men could have more than one). She told them to be good to the children and to all the old people (which is why there were no orphans and all the old people were taken care of and always shown respect).

She stayed with the people four days and taught them how to use the pipe for healing and in seven sacred ceremonies. She left, walking back to the east. She turned into a white buffalo calf (which is why nobody kills a white buffalo calf).

This is the way Flora Driving Hawk would tell the White Buffalo Calf Woman legend. It differs from the way a man would tell the story, barely noting facts important to the men, but stressing those aspects vital to the women. It is an example of the oral tradition on which all North American tribes relied to transmit history and other important cultural elements.

Flora told these stories because they were part of her heritage. She didn't know that they were called *legends* or that they sprang from a people's need to understand, explain, and accept the nature of humankind or the supernatural. At one time they may have had a basis in fact, which over years of retelling has been expanded, distorted, even lost. In my search for my grandmothers, I began with the stories I had heard as a child and read as an adult because they gave me valuable insight into the nature of Indian woman.

Flora was a descendant of the Ring Thunder band of Sicangu Tetons, whose name the French traders translated as "Brulé"—"Burnt," in English. There are several versions of how these people were named, but my favorite is the one Flora told.

They say, long ago before they had horses, the people were on their way home from hunting. It was a good hunt, and everyone carried packs of meat. Even the youngest child who could walk carried a load. The women visited as they walked. They were happy that they had so much good meat and so many hides. It would keep them through the winter.

They walked slowly because of their heavy load. Then a man came racing up, yelling, "Run! There's fire coming!"

Now they ran, but the packs of meat flopped heavily on their backs and slowed them down. They had to throw the meat away. Now the women ran with babies in their arms. The men grabbed up small boys and girls and ran for the creek. But the fire was faster, and before they could reach the water, the fringes on their leggings started smoking. Their moccasins got hot. By the time they got to the creek, they were running through fire.

The men threw the children into the water and pushed the women in, but by the time the men jumped into the water, their leggings and moccasins were burned. They sat in the creek until the fire passed. When they came out of the water, many of the men no longer had moccasins or leggings, and the women's skirts were gone. The fire had burned away their clothes, and their legs were burned all the way to their thighs. This is how the Sicangu, the Burnt Thigh People, got their name.

Flora told other stories to my brother and me, always in the evening. Later I found many of them published in books, ending the illusion that Grandma had created the stories just for us. I was disappointed, even felt betrayed, but then I understood that Grandma's storytelling had been a living of tradition. She did naturally, without conscious thought, what grandmothers were supposed to do.

Flora was also the granddaughter of Mato Wakantuya, High Bear (literally, Call the Name High Bear), and his wife, Skanskanwin, Moving Woman, both full-blood Minneconjous. High Bear was a warrior who, according to Flora, had participated in the Battle of the Little Big Horn. She also said, "They called him a chief," but I had to consult written records to find out more about him.

After the Little Big Horn victory in 1875, the participants had split into bands to evade the U.S. Cavalry and avoid being restricted to the reservation settlements. In early 1877, in a camp on the Little Missouri River north of the Black Hills, High Bear met with other chiefs of the Minneconjou and Sans Arc bands. They talked about the desperate plight of their people, who, in that hard winter, were starving and unable to hunt game because they were pursued by the U.S. Army. It was a difficult and bitter decision the chiefs made to come in to the hated reservation, but in April they surrendered, and High Bear led his family and followers to the Spotted Tail Agency.

High Bear's story led me to further research on the survivors of the Little Big Horn battle, which in turn led me to write my second children's book, *High Elk's Treasure* (1972b). My first children's book, *Jimmy Yellow Hawk* (1972c), was also my first published work.

I had been writing short stories and poetry since high school, and after college I began trying to get published. My theme was Native American aimed at an adult audience, but I found no market for my work. It was only after my daughter Shirley began reading Laura Ingalls Wilder's books that I began writing for children. Shirley was enchanted with the "Little House" books and excited about their South Dakota setting in Desmet, not too far from Brookings, where her father, Vance, grew up. She asked questions about the locale and the early settlers: "Was this the way the Sneve homesteaders lived?"

In order to answer her, I read the books. Always interested in history, I enjoyed them. Then I read *Little House on the Prairie* and found the only reference to Indians in the whole series: "The naked wild men stood by the fireplace. . . . Laura smelled a horrible bad smell. . . . Their faces were bold and fierce" (1971, 137). I wondered what ideas my daughter was acquiring about Indians in the fiction she read. I already knew that she wasn't learning much about them in school; I had taught from the same texts, which either ignored their place in American history or briefly mentioned the wars and how "savages" hindered western movement. I began to read children's literature and found that Indians were a popular theme, but always Indians of the past—brave boy warriors and cute princesses, or brutal savages. I found no stories of modern Indian children.

How did my children view their Indian relatives from where we lived in Cedar Rapids, Iowa? My mother and brother no longer lived on South Dakota reservations, and our visits were only a few days in the summer—usually during the Rosebud Fair or Sun Dance time. We'd make a stop to see Grandma Driving Hawk, then go on to Uncle Harvey's in Pine Ridge. My son, Paul, was fascinated with Uncle Harvey, who worked in the maintenance department at the Pine Ridge School, where, Agnes, his wife, taught. On one visit Harvey had given Paul a picture of himself wearing a wig with braids hanging over a breastplate. Paul hung the picture in his room and proudly displayed it to his four-year-old friends. Unbeknownst to me, Paul told his pals that Harvey hunted buffalo from a horse and was a fierce warrior.

Uncle Harvey and Aunt Agnes were coming to visit us, and Paul eagerly anticipated their arrival. He and several of his buddies camped on the edge of our driveway to welcome Harvey, who came riding up in an air-conditioned automobile wearing a sports shirt, slacks, and shoes.

Later, a mother of one of the boys told me that they had been furious with Paul. Harvey wasn't an Indian; he looked just like Vance, Paul's dad.

This was in the 1960s, when the nation's racial conscience was being challenged by the demands of black Americans for civil rights. In the 1970s, we had moved to Flandreau, South Dakota, where Vance and I taught at the Indian High School. AIM, the American Indian Movement, was flourishing and occupied Wounded Knee. The American Indian became a Native American, and there was a demand for truthful ethnic stories for children written by minority writers. The Interracial Council of Minority Books for Children, made up of publishers, editors, and writers, sponsored an annual contest to encourage minority writers to write for children.

I submitted *Jimmy Yellow Hawk*, a story of a modern Sioux boy on a South Dakota reservation. It was based on my brother's brief attempts at fur trapping along the Little Oak Creek. The manuscript won the Native American category and was published by Holiday House in New York, with whom I would have a twenty-year association.

I was in a fortunate position to meet the demand for works by Native American authors. Unknowingly, I had prepared myself to write for children by reading their literature; I knew what had been printed and what needed to be published. I had taken a writing course at Iowa State College to renew my teaching certificate; then, when we returned to South Dakota, I enrolled in a research methods class as part of my graduate studies at South Dakota State University. Now, in South Dakota, close to my roots among the western Sioux, I searched for a subject for my second children's book. After a visit to Grandma Driving Hawk, I asked her about High Bear being part of the Little Big Horn battle. To my disappointment, she responded only, "That's what they said." She knew nothing more. I began the research and found nothing of High Bear in the literature on the battle, but I did find a brief mention of a group of Sioux and Chey-enne warriors who took a vow of silence not to reveal which of them had killed General Custer. The vow extended to their descendants and would last for one hundred years. This became the basis for *High Elk's Treasure*, a story of a western Sioux family's life after the victory at the Little Big Horn.

It was after the Little Big Horn battle that the western Sioux tribes had to reside within reservation boundaries. Before that, the Minneconjous and others had a short, gloriously exciting life after they crossed the Missouri River into a land of extremes: blizzards, thunder- and hailstorms, perpetual winds, heat, drought, floods, and bitter cold. Yet the wide expanse of prairie rolling to the sacred Black Hills had the beauty of unlimited horizons; it was the domain of the horsemen. In *High Elk's Treasure* I wrote of how the modern Sioux had retained their love of horses even though they now had a sedentary reservation life.

The Minneconjous, whose name indicates that they had once planted crops by water, willingly gave up the life of the wood-lands for the richness and glory of painted men and horses, brave warriors in flowing headdresses whose mates were strong, hand-some women. The Minneconjou and other western Sioux women determinedly adapted to this new life to ensure the survival of their children.

It was a glorious culture of dreams and song. Reckless deeds were performed by brave warriors who thought striking a live enemy more honorable than killing, an act the French called *coup*. Skanskan-win was wooed by such a warrior, who serenaded her with his flute until she allowed him to stand close within the shelter of her blanket. Mato Wakantuya brought horses, which Skanskanwin's father ac-cepted, and thus the young couple were wed.

Flora told legends of youthful love and heartbreak in that storied time, and I was enthralled with the romance of them.

> They say, there was a war party on a butte. Their enemy was all around them, and they couldn't get down. They all died up there. Many years later, the people of the same tribe camped near that same butte. One woman left her husband's tepee and walked to the top. She pulled her shawl over her head and sang about the man she had loved who had died there. All the while she sang, she was dancing backward. She danced to the edge of the butte and fell over.

She was dead, but her husband didn't want her body. He hadn't known that his wife loved the other man, and he was jealous. Her relatives took her body to the top of the butte. They laid her down on top of all those bones up there. Ever since, no one goes to that place because the ghosts of that woman and man are up there.

Another tale was of a woman who was unhappy when her husband brought home a second wife.

She couldn't stay there with that new wife, so she ran away. She walked for many days along Cherry Creek. There used to be lots of wolves along the creek, but the woman wasn't scared. She was so tired from walking that she lay down and went to sleep in the grass.

She woke up, and her face felt warm and wet. There was a she-wolf licking her face. The she-wolf led the woman to a cave, and she lived in that cave with the wolves for a long time.

But she got lonesome for people, and when some Sicangus went by, she went with them to the Rosebud reservation. The family named Grey Wolf comes from the woman who lived with the wolves.

This tale reminded Flora of another involving women and an animal.

Some women were picking berries on a hot day when a bear came into the woods. All the women ran, but one old woman was too slow, and the bear knocked her down with one slap of his paw. The bear ran after the others and struck another woman. He tried to turn her over, but she had fallen with her body all bent over double. She reached for her knife and stabbed the bear. The bear staggered a ways and then fell down dead. From then on the brave woman was called Bear Woman.

Women had special missions, as shown in the legend of the young Buffalo Calf Woman and also in another tale that Flora related about an aged, nameless woman.

They say, that an old woman and her dog live out in the Badlands. She sits on the ground with little piles of colored quills spread on a hide. She is decorating a robe with a pretty quillwork design. She gets tired sitting like that, so every so often she has to get up to stretch. Sometimes when she gets up, she goes to fix her fire so it won't go out. All the while the dog

watches her. When she is busy fixing the fire, the dog gets up—
he stretches too—then goes to the robe and pulls out the quills.
This way, the work is never done. If the woman ever finishes her
quillwork, it will be the end of the world.

These are just a few of the stories Flora told, but from them I
learned that Indian women were passionate and jealous, sometimes
resorting to suicide because they could not live without their lovers.
I also knew that even after settlement on the reservations some
women killed themselves out of lovesick despair and that it was not
uncommon for a woman to run away from a loveless marriage.
Flora's legends also showed that women were resourceful and brave,
as in the encounters with animals, but, most significantly, that ancient
western Sioux woman is credited with controlling the continuation
of life itself and the younger Buffalo Calf Woman with giving direction to the way that life should be lived.

Flora's grandmother, Skanskanwin, lived the life enjoined by the
White Buffalo Calf Woman, during a time when "not only the honor,
but the very existence of the tribe lay in the moccasin tracks of their
women" (Sandoz 1967, 72–73). Indeed, the earth on which the moccasins trod was female: "O You, Mother Earth, who bear and nourish
all fruits, behold us and listen: Upon You there is a sacred path which
we walk, thinking of the sacredness of all things" (Brown 1971, 133).

This era of the Tetons' time on Mother Earth was often glorious,
and Skanskanwin knew its bounty. It was a time of change, and the
people adapted traditional customs to meet new needs. For example,
before the dog was used as a pack animal, every able person walked
when a band was on the move, and the women carried the babies
plus all the camp equipment. The men aligned themselves at the
front, rear, and sides of the march to keep an eye out for game and to
protect the helpless—the women, children, and elders. This strategy
of travel prevailed until some weary woman seeking to ease her
burden fashioned a drag for the dog to pull. Two dogs were trained
to work as a team to transport the ill and the infirm elderly. This drag,
called a *travois* by the French, was quickly adapted for use with the
horse.

The larger travois and the horse made the women's travel lighter
and more efficient, and the whole band could move more quickly.
During the peak of the nomadic buffalo culture, every adult and
child who was able had a horse to ride, for it was a shameful thing

for a man to be unable to provide horses for each member of his household.

Domestic chores often involved hard physical labor for Skanskanwin and other prereservation homemakers, but they did not consider their tasks drudgery. Polygamy—a practice that most whites found reprehensible—lessened an individual wife's duties. The more wives a man had, the more skins could be tanned for the comfort of the lodge; however, the more women in the lodge, the more they controlled the man. Not every woman, as legends show, wanted to share her husband with another woman. A few chose suicide; many more left their men, taking with them their possessions and children (who were considered to "belong" to the mother). Such a woman was usually welcome to return to her parents' home, where her father, if able, provided for her. If he could not, the woman's brothers or male cousins assumed the responsibility until she remarried.

Flora did not know whether her grandfather, Mato Wakantuya, had more than one wife; she spoke only of Skanskanwin, whose name is recorded as "High Bear's wife" in the Rosebud Episcopal Mission register. Men often married sisters, an arrangement meant to keep peace in the lodge, but one that was not always successful. Sometimes the older sister was jealous of the younger or the younger thought the older too bossy. Sometimes one thought the husband favored the other. Then they would argue and fight until the husband intervened to restore peace.

What Flora did know was that there were distinct roles for Skanskanwin and Mato Wakantuya and that neither thought one's duties of lesser worth than the other's. Mato Wakantuya was an expert horseman and brave warrior and hunter. He killed buffalo, which then became Skanskanwin's to skin and butcher. She cooked and served the meat and dried the surplus for later use. She worked the hides into robes to be used as beds, blankets, carpets, moccasins, and storage containers. The tough strips of sinew she used as lacing to bind hides together into large, sturdy shelters. The buffalo enriched the plains Indians' lives, but it was the woman like Skanskanwin who made it so.

Skanskanwin cared for her lodge, and its contents were hers, as were the children, whom she treasured. When Mato Wakantuya was not away hunting or waging war, he was a father who took time to play with and sing to his young children. He was also thoughtful and considerate of Skanskanwin and she of him. They addressed each other with fond respect; to him Skanskanwin was *mitawicu*, "my wife"; she called him *mihigna*, "my husband." They openly demonstrated their affection in the daily act of combing and braiding each other's hair.

Skanskanwin did not consider herself exploited by this seemingly lopsided share of duties but was content to be provided for and protected by her husband, whose prowess in battle and the hunt brought esteem to her family.

Later, as I had for the legends Flora told, I found that the written record of this oral lore applied to all Sioux men and women: "Women and children were the objects of care among the Lakotas and as far as their environment permitted they lived sheltered lives. Life was softened by a great equality. All the tasks of women—cooking, caring for children, tanning and sewing—were considered dignified and worthwhile. No work was looked upon as menial, consequently there were no menial workers. Industry filled the life of every Lakota woman" (Standing Bear 1931, 64).

And the women shared their labors. Women of one family worked together and also helped women of other families in moving camp (dismantling and setting up the tepees), in midwifery, and in the technical and artistic knowledge of tanning and constructing lodge covers, clothing, quillwork, and beadwork. Even as they toiled, the women delighted in the sociability of female companionship, and they cared for each other's children. Ella Deloria wrote of this in *Waterlily*, relating a women's berry-picking expedition:

> The women had organized into *tiyospaye* groups, or into congenial parties of friends from here and there who wished to spend the day together and make of the communal enterprise a sociable excursion as well. At sunrise they went out and set up their awnings all along the first shelf of land above the valley floor where the silvery-leafed bushes grew thick. They spread blankets about and set their drinking water and food under the shades. There they left one or two of their party to look after things and keep an eye on the babies and small children who could not walk far. (1988b, 222)

All adults watched over the children, on whom the tribe's survival depended. Rarely was an infant apart from its mother; the babe was either carried on its mother's back or securely placed in a cradleboard, always within view. When this wasn't possible, it was the duty of an older sister or brother to watch over the younger ones. The birth of a girl was no less welcome than that of a boy, for she had the power of life within her; the continuity of the tribe's existence rested with her, as the White Buffalo Calf Woman had ordained.

Skanskanwin would have felt as Deloria's Waterlily did. " 'All my relatives are noble,' she thought. 'They make of their duties toward others a privilege and a delight. It was no struggle to play one's kinship role with people like them. When everyone was up to par in this kinship interchange of loyalty and mutual dependence, life could be close to perfect.' " (1988, 224).

Skanskanwin and all women were highly esteemed in the tribe, and it was important that young girls behave in such a manner as not to betray that esteem. In *Speaking of Indians,* Deloria wrote of the instruction given in the Buffalo Ceremony held at the time of a girl's becoming a woman: "A real woman is virtuous and soft-spoken and modest and does not shame her husband and neglect her children. She is skillful in the womanly arts and hospitable to all who enter her dwelling. She remains at home ready to receive guests at all times. Her fire burns permanently cheery and smoke curls prettily upward from her tipi-head" (1988a, 65).

A giveaway was held in the girl's honor, with her brothers and cousins giving gifts in her name. But if the girl forgot her instructions and acted foolishly, she was reminded by her mother or grandmother, "Your brothers and cousins gave away many fine horses in your honor. Can it be that they acted so nobly all in vain?" (Deloria 1988a, 65). A young girl's tarnished reputation shamed not only her but all her relatives.

In her full and busy life, Skanskanwin found time to make and adorn all the clothing she wore. Her skin skirt was sewn on two sides with fringes in the seams and across the bottom that swayed across her leggings. Her upper garment was capelike, covering her shoulders and the upper part of her arms. Her hair was long, sometimes worn loose, or braided and tied with bits of leather or, later, ribbon. In her ears she wore brass wire earrings.

Skanskanwin took great pride in her appearance and that of her family, whose apparel she also made. Indeed, her family's well-being was of the utmost importance to her, and her summers were spent in continual efforts to ensure the survival of her family and tribe during the lean winter. Besides processing meat and hides after the buffalo hunts, she gathered and dried berries and wild vegetables to supplement the high-protein diet.

After Skanskanwin and other women picked choke cherries, they spread the fruit to dry in the sun. When it was thoroughly dried, she pounded it together with bits of dried meat, blending the mixture with suet. This she rolled into egg-sized balls or patties, which were relished as her grandchildren would learn to savor candy.

Sometimes Skanskanwin boiled the fresh or dried berries into a tart juice, which she thickened with the flour made from the wild prairie turnip, *tipsila*. Modern Sioux women still pick and dry choke cherries and dig the prairie turnip. They prepare *tipsila* in the same way as Skanskanwin might have done: fresh in a soup of meat and corn, or pounded into a flour, or dried and stored for winter use.

Just as Skanskanwin prepared for winter, she taught her daughter, Pejuta Okawin, who in turn trained her daughter, Flora, who knew where to find the wild turnip and showed me, her granddaughter, how to braid it into long strings to dry in the sun and wind.

Skanskanwin's world was not all romantic glory; she also knew physical hardship and life-threatening danger from humans and nature. Flora's stories told of fire, war, and encounters with animals, all of which I found vividly depicted in winter counts.

Winter counts were a method of recording a people's story that the western Sioux tribes used to augment the telling. The recorders of the winter counts used this prewriting method of drawing pictographic symbols to represent an event for a particular year, thus annually recording history. A study of the interpretation of three winter counts of the western Sioux spanning 181 years shows events concerning women depicted twenty-one times and another thirteen symbolic events related to children (see "Big Missouri Winter Count" 1973; Robinson 1925; and Young Bear 1987).

In the winter counts reproduced in table 1 are three entries concerning death from disease: in 1780, smallpox was very bad; in 1860, many infants died in an epidemic; and in 1861, many children died of an unknown disease. Children were the precious reason for a tribe's existence, and in times when food was scarce, adults went without to ensure the survival of the children and, thus, the tribe. The deaths of many children from strange illnesses—smallpox, cholera, measles, chicken pox, whooping cough—diseases unknown to the New World until brought by Europeans, decimated many tribes. Skanskanwin's

Table 1: Winter Counts

	Robinson 1775–1885	Spider's 1759–1956	Big Missouri 1796–1926
1780	Smallpox very bad.		
1784	A captive Omaha woman tried to escape, but was killed.		
1792	Many women died in childbirth.		
1793	A captive Ponca boy killed by his own people.		
1798	An Arikara woman was digging turnips. A captured enemy woman claimed to be a spirit.		
1799	Many women died in childbirth.	Many pregnant women died.	A very cold winter caused the death of many expectant women.
1804	An unfaithful woman was killed by a man named Ponca.		
1805			A delegation of Indians and their wives went to Washington.
1828			A woman, abused by her husband, fled to her father, Walking Crow. Her husband pursued her, attacked the father, then returned

Table 1: *Continued*

	Robinson 1775–1885	Spider's 1759–1956	Big Missouri 1796–1926
			to his own tepee. The father followed and shot and killed him.
1834			A Cheyenne, married to a Sioux girl during peace, deserted her when war began between the tribes. After the war, he returned, but the Sioux killed him.
1838	Iron Horn, father of Mrs. Frederick Dupree, built a dirt lodge on the Moreau River.		A man from Broken Bow's camp stole a wife from another camp. This caused such bad feeling that the Broken Bow man was killed.
1847	Big Thunder's wife bore twins.		Tall Joe, a white man, and his Sioux wife's grown son were drowned.
1850			An old woman was found dead in a buffalo carcass.
1857			A Crow woman was killed by the Sioux.
1860		Many infants died in an epidemic.	
1861			Many children died of an unknown disease.

Table 1: *Continued*

	Robinson *1775–1885*	Spider's *1759–1956*	Big Missouri *1796–1926*
1862		A young boy was scalped.	
1869			The first child enters school.
1883			Dog Shield died. His grieving wife hanged herself. They were buried together.
1887			Two women had bloated stomachs from an unknown ailment. The agency doctor tapped their stomachs, but they died.
1891			Two head of cattle issued to every man, woman, and child.
1905		Gray Bonnet's child committed suicide.	Leader Charger's wife gave birth to quadruplets.
1913		First schools on Pine Ridge.	
1919			Two girls ran away from St. Francis School on a cold day. One froze to death; the other's feet were amputated.
1920		Young girl drowned.	

Table 1: *Continued*

	Robinson 1775–1885	Spider's 1759–1956	Big Missouri 1796–1926
1921			Two boys ran away from St. Francis School on a cold day. One froze to death. The other lived.
1925		Red Shirt and his child died.	

people were familiar with the white men who came to trade, and with them came diseases for which the medicine men had no cure. Roaming bands like Skanskanwin's found silent villages of the dead and dying, victims of these deadly diseases, abandoned by their frightened families. Skanskanwin may have witnessed the terror and known the distress of being unable to aid the helpless victims:

> A young mother was left in her lodge with her small child, and she soon succumbed, a victim to the dreadful disease. A bedraggled band happened to pass through this deserted village where pitiful sights confronted them. Within the lodge, with its side rolled up, was revealed a child nursing its dead mother. For fear of being exposed [to the disease], this one pitiful case and others in the same plight were left to combat their own perils. Occasionally some afflicted person would wander in view of an Indian village. He would at once sound a warning with one hand elevated, denoting that he was exposed. Food and other nourishment would be placed in a vacant lodge, and the occupants would flee for other parts. The contagious epidemic practically wiped out one-third of their population. The dreadful disease did not subside until cold weather set in. This was the most violent form of smallpox. (Bordeaux 1929, 20)

Cholera found its way to the western tribes via emigrants following the Overland Trail in the mid-1800s, and, in the Fort Laramie area, it was one of the reasons the Indians became increasingly fearful and distrustful of whites. The winter counts named only smallpox as a cause of death from disease, but the reason for the deaths of pregnant women in 1792 and 1799 is not known. The loss of child-bearing women and the unborn children was, however, a double disaster.

In the winter counts there are two notations of multiple births: in 1849, Big Thunder's wife bore twins; in 1905, Leader Charger's wife gave birth to quadruplets. The birth of twins was rare and an occasion of great excitement and wonder; the birth of quadruplets must have caused agitation of earthquake proportions.

When twins were born, it was fortuitous if both lived, for it was thought that the two, while in the womb, fought about which would be born first. The stronger of the two always won the right to be the eldest, and the weaker baby pouted after birth and frequently died. Thus, twins who survived were *wakan* (holy or spiritual) and reverently respected all their lives. It was unheard of for even one of triplets or quadruplets to live more than a few days.

Violent deaths of children, be they from accident, murder, or suicide, were extreme oddities for a people whose extended family system ensured that children were sheltered and protected at all times. In 1793, a Ponca boy who had been a captive was killed by his own people, an event of horrifying rarity. Perhaps the boy's death was accidental, or did the Ponca consider captivity by the Sioux too abhorrent even to reclaim one of their own? The 1862 depiction of a boy being scalped was equally shocking, for such acts were considered worthy only if the victim was an adult warrior. Perhaps it was deviant behavior of a deranged person, or perhaps it was done by a white man.

The records of women in the winter counts indicate that they committed suicide and that they were taken captive, but rarely were women killed—even unfaithful wives. Only later, on the reservations, did murder—of both sexes and all ages—become a frequent crime. Written records also note that husbands punished an unfaithful wife by shaving her head from the nape of the neck to the brow, mutilating her arms and hands, and slashing her shoulder blades (Tabeau 1968, 178–79).

Unfaithful men did not suffer the same public humiliation; indeed, a man was thought to be more manly if he successfully seduced another's wife. But if the husband's philandering became so blatant as to cause embarrassment and shame to the wife's family, she could leave him and take the children with her. However, Flora's oral history recounted, "My aunt's husband was always after other women—everyone knew, and my aunt was shamed. One night he didn't come home and she knew he'd been with some woman, so she waited and as soon as he got in the door, she chased him out with her ax."

Other angry wives took after their philandering husbands with their butcher knives. Or, as Flora told, continuing her aunt's story, "He still went after other women, so my aunt told her brothers. They got mad and waited for him to come home. Here he come, all pleased with himself, but the brothers beat him up."

The old woman found dead in a buffalo carcass in the winter count entry for 1850 may have been caught in a winter storm and been resourceful enough to find shelter in the warm carcass of a freshly killed buffalo, an act often recounted in oral stories. Unfortunately, winter storms frequently lasted many days, accompanied by severe cold, and when the carcass froze, death found the individual sheltered within. Or the old woman may have been left behind in a storm because she was ill and chose to stay rather than endanger her family by her weakness. Or it may have been one of the rare cases where an old woman had no one to care for her and she survived as best she could.

The winter counts are a prewriting history of the culture and life that Skanskanwin knew until it all changed with the coming of the white men, fur traders, who took Indian women as wives.

The white traders my western Sioux ancestors met were French men from St. Louis, and one of the first things they and other French men did was obtain a wife. Sometimes these men had a wife in each of the tribes with which they dealt, or married sisters, or had several wives in one tribe. There were also Spanish and Anglo-Saxon traders who sired mixed-blood children by Indian women. These children not only had mixed blood but also grew up experiencing a blend of customs and values. My own multicultural heritage has lent that theme to my writing.

This diverse melding began with the union of several of my grandmothers with white men who came as fur traders. These liaisons were a mixed blessing, bringing many new and useful goods to the tribes, but also other new products, customs, and diseases that proved disastrous.

My great-grandmother, Pejuta Okawin, daughter of Skanskanwin and Mato Wakantuya, married a mixed blood. Her name, Pejuta Okawin, meant "All around Medicine Woman" and was given to her because of her skill in using medicinal plants to treat wounds and illness. After her baptism on Christmas Day, 1898, in the Episcopal Church of Jesus at the Rosebud Agency, she was called "Lucy." She was married in a church ceremony on 12 March 1898 to James Clairmont, mixed-blood son of Henri Clairmont, a French man from St. Louis.

Henri, listed in the 1880 census as Henry Clairmont, white male, born in Missouri to parents who were born in France, was a fur trader who operated a post at the Whetstone Agency on the Missouri River. On 20 July 1874, he married a full-blood Sicangu (or Brulé), whose name was recorded in Episcopal church records as "Emily." Emily was the sister of Chan Gleska Wakinyan, Ring Thunder, a Brulé chief.

Another French trader, Antoine Dubray, contributed to my diverse heritage, with his union with Louise Robinson (Robeson). Louise, the second of three daughters of William Robeson and Susan Alice Paladay, was born near the North Platte. Louise (with "Pine Ridge" after her name in Bureau of Indian Affairs records) was the product of a white-Indian liaison, and her father, William, is believed to have been in the fur trade in the Fort John (Laramie) area.

Antoine was from Missouri and with the American Fur Company in the Rockies in about 1828. *Dubray* is believed to be a corruption of the French *Du Breuil*. According to one family story, the nickname "Chat" or "Chet" was given him from *le chat* for his cat-like manner of movement. According to another family tale, the nickname may have come from *le chateau Dubray*, after his trading post on the Missouri River near the Whetstone Agency. "Chet," as he was most commonly called, was an employee at Bent's Fort during the 1840s. He may also have lived among the Arapahoes.

Dubray had four wives, after the Indian custom. Family lore holds that Louise was the second wife, Fatura Ducharme the first, and Julia Moran and Jennie Bissionette third and fourth. However, Louise, Fatura, and Julia may have been "sister-wives" because their children by Antoine were born from 1856 to 1876. Whether they all lived with him at the same location is not known. Fatura may have divorced him. Family history has it that Louise was with Antoine at the Whetstone Agency, but perhaps Julia was also.

Traders Henri Clairmont and Antoine Dubray moved with their Indian families to the Whetstone Agency, on the Missouri River, where the Brulé, under the leadership of Sinte Gleska, Spotted Tail, were first settled. However, the Brulé would be moved seven times more before permanently settling at Rosebud in 1878.

Enoch Wheeler Raymond, who was the first agent at Whetstone from June to December 1868 (*Tripp County South Dakota* 1984, 14), also had a mixed-blood wife, Elizabeth Papin. Elizabeth certainly knew Louise, one of Antoine Dubray's wives, and Emily, the wife of Henri Clairmont, who were among the seventy-nine "French Indians" or "squaw men" living at Whetstone. Flora, Henri's granddaughter, said that he had a trading post at Whetstone, which is marked on the map of the agency as "Mr. Claymore." Because they had married Indian women, Henri and the other white men were considered members of the tribe, were entitled to all annuities and rations, and later were allotted land.

Captain D. C. Poole, the next agent at Whetstone, described the location at the mouth of Whetstone Creek on the Missouri River:

> The "first bench," or level ground extending immediately back from the river, was some eighty rods wide, and covered in most places with a thick growth of willows interlaced with wild vines. A sharp rise of six or eight feet led to the "second bench," another level stretch of ground which extended back to the bluffs, covered near the river with an undergrowth of oak, but soon running into prairie. This rich bottom land followed the course of the river for some four miles, but was cut off above and below by the bluffs, which at these points circled into the very bank. Whetstone Creek, fringed with a very small growth of timber, broke through the range of bluffs from the west and joined the Missouri, while farther south Scalp Creek did the same.... An island in the river, a short distance from the agency, furnished cottonwood logs for fuel and for building.
>
> Near the edge of the second bench a row of rough log buildings was ranged, the carpenter's shop, blacksmith's shop, two medium sized storehouses, an office and council room in one, a dispensary, the barn and stables, and, to the left and towards the river, the saw mill....
>
> The rest of the ground back to the bluffs was occupied by Indian Tepees. The trader's store, holding a central position, was by far the most pretentious building of all. (Poole [1881] 1988, 29–30)

The tepees around the store were no longer constructed of buffalo hides but were made instead from white canvass as part of the annuity goods issued the Brulé. One shipment of supplies also contained 256 wool blankets, which replaced the buffalo robes, and 548 yards of calico, which took the place of buckskin garments. Emily Clairmont and Louise Dubray, along with the other women, fashioned the calico into the long, shapeless gown that would become the traditional dress of Indian women and is still worn by older Indian women today.

At Whetstone, "women's day" was the day rations were distributed at the agency. Near the commissary building, my grandmothers aligned themselves with the other women at the front of the large circle formed by all the agency Indians. The white employees brought out the rations and piled them in the center of the circle, to the delight of the women. The women chattered and murmured with pleasure, words that turned to a Lakota song giving employees descriptive Indian names:

> See, See, Red Head brings the sides of bacon;
> See, see, Big Nose brings the bags of beans;
> Now comes Little White Man with the sugar sacks;
> Chatka is carrying the coffee bags! (Poole 1988, 55)

At Whetstone, the Indians were expected to farm, but the nomadic tribes had long given up any semblance of farming, and what was done, was done by the women. The male Indian had no interest in plowing the garden even though in each council meeting the men were repeatedly reminded by Poole "of the desire of their Great Father [the president] that they should learn to cultivate the soil" (Poole 1988, 55). The men, who never allowed their women to listen to council meetings, agreed with the agent—and turned the work over to the women.

The women planted corn, pumpkins, squash, and beans in the spring, then went off with their men to hunt, only to find on their return in late summer that drought had destroyed the crop. The only successful gardens were the plots planted along the river by Emily Clairmont or Louise Dubray along with the women of other white men. Their relatives may not have farmed themselves but could be counted on to gather round the productive gardens to share in the harvest.

In addition to the smaller plots, the agent had plowed a large common field, a forerunner of the communal gardens of the 1930s. The agency farm "showed a sickly array of the products of husbandry," Poole wrote, describing wheat that, "having attained a height of four or five inches, head out and completed its growth in this dwarfed state; the straw being so short that it could not be harvested with the approved machine" (Poole 1988, 37). The Ree or squaw corn, adapted to the climate, did better, until the grasshoppers arrived to strip the stalks.

Also at Whetstone at the same time as Emily and Henri Clairmont and the Dubray women was another Brulé ancestress, Mary Comes Out. Mary was the wife of Gustavus Butler, who was murdered in his sleep at the Whetstone Agency the day after Christmas, 1875. Mary would later marry a Scots trader, Joseph Ross.

Mary Comes Out, Emily Ring Thunder, and Louise Robeson undoubtedly knew each other at the Whetstone Agency, where they cared for their white husbands as they would have an Indian one and their female relatives helped with the traders' furs. They were a liaison with the white world through their husbands, who often served as interpreters and tribal advocates. Through these alliances, traders Henri Clairmont and Antoine Dubray also benefited in acquiring an extended family with tribal affiliation to ensure their economic success. These French men adopted the Lakota language and Lakota customs; indeed, they were often called *French Indians*.

Anglo-Saxon men like Gustavus Butler and Joseph Ross were more likely to retain their cultural identities, and their Indian wives became bilingual and had to adapt to their husbands' lifestyles. These men were called *squaw men*, which, along with *French Indian*, was a derogatory label given by white society, which generally thought of Indian women as fiendishly immoral snares who entrapped civilized men.

Dubray, Clairmont, and Ross were just three of thousands of white men lured west by the fur trade who cohabited with, had children by, and sometimes legally married Indian women.

My grandmothers, and other Indian women who were the first of their tribes to cohabit with white men, brought honor to their families and tribes by doing so. But they, like other Indian wives of white men, soon found that their lives were filled with drudgery if there were no "sister-wife" to share the household and conjugal duties. A single wife gave birth more frequently and over a longer period of time and, as a result, suffered more in childbirth.

By the 1850s, all the tribes were distrustful of the whites, and a woman married to a white was lowered in status and frequently lived apart from her nomadic family. If she were physically abused, there were no brothers to protect her, no family to shelter her if she ran away. In the early fur trade years, such a woman and her children were welcomed back into the family circle, but later she became an outcast as her former alliance was considered shameful. The most difficult aspect for these women to accept was that all the goods in the house were the property of the man; therefore, she lost control of her home and of her children.

With the advent of the fur trade, these changes led to the deterioration of the female's status as husbands began bartering the pelts their wives had tanned for guns and whiskey. Later, at Fort Laramie, the Indian relatives of women married to traders became dependent on trade goods and whiskey, no longer hunting to supply food, clothing, or shelter. These Indians called *fort Indians*, or *waglukhe*, became known in written history as the "Loafer band" among the Brulé. Bands such as High Bear's and others still living the nomadic life scorned these "hang-around-the-fort" Indians and those who had moved to the reservation at Whetstone.

Fort Laramie, best known as the site of treaty negotiations, is infamous in oral history for the alcohol-related abuse of women that occurred there. Alcohol also caused problems at Whetstone and was supplied by the traders Dubray and Clairmont. Gustavus Butler may have been murdered as a result of a drunken spree among the Indians. As Indian men became addicted to alcohol, fathers, brothers, and husbands traded their daughters, sisters, and wives for whiskey. The whiskey trade got so bad that Spotted Tail requested "soldiers kept at Laramie and also on the Missouri River [Whetstone] to keep off bad whites and whiskey" (Welsh 1870, 17).

The military presence in the West resulted in large numbers of fatherless half-breed children born as the result of alcoholic trade or prostitution but also as the result of rape during and after military engagements. To celebrate a victory, troopers often rounded up the prettiest girls to be passed among the officers, leaving the enlisted men with the less attractive, older women. After the decline of the fur trade, many of the traders stayed with their Indian wives and children, but many more returned to civilization, either abandoning wives and children or leaving the wife and taking the children to be raised as whites. Some traders took only the male children or sent half-breed sons back East to be educated, but, as adults, these sons often returned to their mothers' tribes to live as Indians.

In Dakota, there were large numbers of "French Indians" like Henry Clairmont and Chet Dubray who established trading posts along the rivers and who stayed with their Indian families. They, their women, and their children were counted in the 1859 census. In 1862, the General Half-Breed Bill was introduced in the territorial legislature with the provisions being that all English-language literate mixed bloods would be granted citizenship; however, it was defeated because "under the act the half-breeds would have outvoted all the rest of the territory" (Armstrong 1901, 73). By 1870, the population of Dakota Territory seemed to have exploded because the large numbers of mixed-blood offspring—who were more numerous than the whites—had been counted.

Spotted Tail was concerned with the welfare of his people at Whetstone, and he requested a missionary from the Episcopal Church, "as I find out it will be for the good of my people, and my white relations [traders] have recommended it" (Welsh 1870, 17).

Spotted Tail's tribe and the western Sioux knew of Christianity from Father Pierre Jean DeSmet, a Belgian priest who kept records of baptisms and marriages among them. He reminded the French traders of their Catholic heritage, and if they did not always marry their Indian wives, they made sure that their half-breed children were baptized.

Spotted Tail's people and other western tribes managed in their own fashion to fit the values of the old into Christianity and understood, by their knowledge of the Sun Dance, the asceticism and the torture of the Crucifixion for the good of others. Giving to others, especially to the poor, was common to them. The high honor that Christianity accorded virginity was similar to the White Buffalo Calf Woman's decree. Putting money in the collection plate was a semblance of giving honor to another person and gaining prestige in the Sioux giveaway pattern.

Later, in 1874, Bishop Hare and Samuel Hinman visited Spotted Tail, and Hare wrote, "This is one of the finest opportunities for the establishment of the Church and the preaching of the Gospel that I ever saw" (1874, 19). Hare was referring not only to the Indians but to the many white men who had Indian wives and their half-breed children.

It was on this visit in July 1874 that Hinman performed ceremonies legalizing the marriages of a number of the traders and their

Indian wives, including my great-great-grandparents, Henry and Emily Clairmont.

Because the Indians could leave Whetstone to hunt, the white citizens of Dakota Territory were afraid of them wandering wherever they pleased. The territorial government attempted to enforce an 1863 law that forbade Indians entering ceded territorial land without a written pass from their agent. Any found without the pass would be subject to arrest by county authorities and returned to the proper reservation. The U.S. Indian agent would reimburse the county in which the arrest was made for the expenses incurred. The Whetstone Indians either did not know of the law or ignored it and still moved freely to hunt and visit other tribes.

In 1870, Spotted Tail left Whetstone to visit the Santee reservation in Nebraska and was impressed with the apparently peaceful existence that the "praying Santee" had adopted—they had a school, a chapel, a hospital, wagons, and horses. But he was also saddened that these Indians were becoming imitation whites.

KUNSI

Kunsi, great grandmother in her hard chair,
hands busy at her cross stitch.
We, at her feet, reluctantly
needlepointing crooked crosses.
Rocker creaking to Kunsi's stern
command to remember Minnesota exiles
starving, dying, and surviving Crow Creek
to live again at Santee.
History she told, but thoughtless
children wanted to be entertained.
from "Story Tellers"

In my childhood Kunsi was my great-grandmother, Hannah Howe Frazier. She was a mixed-blood Ponca who knew not only of her own tribe's history but also of the Santees' through her marriage to a Santee. Hannah was a stern but devout Christian whom I respected with fearful, almost reverent awe.

It was in the early 1940s in Okreek, South Dakota, that I came to know Hannah after she was widowed and living with her daughter Harriet. During those years, when my parents were away at summer jobs needed to supplement Dad's salary as a priest of the Episcopal Church, my brother Edward and I alternated summers at Okreek with summers at the Driving Hawks' in Mission, which was sixteen miles west of Okreek on Highway 16.

Grandmother Harriet Ross was a busy woman caring for two children still at home and her husband and mother, but if the addition of two active grandchildren was a strain on her already busy days, we never knew it. As I look back, however, I realize that was why we spent so much time with Great-grandmother.

Hannah's storytelling was done in the afternoon, during the time to be quiet, probably giving Harriet a chance to rest. I remember sitting on the floor at Hannah's feet, struggling with some handwork, embroidery or crochet, because she believed that "idle hands make work for the devil." To this day I cannot sit idly relaxed without a craft project in my hands, even while watching television.

In the midst of instruction or assistance with the embroidery, Hannah told about the Poncas and the Santees. Hannah's grandmother was Shots through the Breast, a mixed-blood Ponca, daughter of White Woman, who Hannah said was a "chieftess." The story of White Woman is family legend.

Long ago two young Ponca girls, one the chief's daughter, were taken captive by an enemy band of the Crow tribe and taken far into the north. They were reared as Crow women and learned the art of tanning buckskin so that it was beautifully white.

Even though the girls were well treated, they never forgot their Ponca families and home along the Missouri River. After a while the girls were no longer carefully guarded, and one of the girls escaped.

This was in the time before the horse, so the girl ran all night to gain distance from her captors, who either did not pursue her or did not catch her because she was far away. She traveled south until she came to familiar landmarks along the Missouri River and found her way to a Ponca village. All night she watched the village to be sure it was safe and saw that there was great activity in and around the chief's lodge, her father's home. As the sun rose, the girl stood and showed herself to the people, who were surprised and awed by the sight of this lovely young woman whose buckskin garment gleamed radiantly white in the bright rays of the rising sun.

After she identified herself and was recognized by her relatives, she was told that her father had died and that the nightlong activity at his lodge was indecisive debate to choose his successor. She told them of her captivity and daring escape, and this, coupled with her spectacular reappearance in the village, caused the people to believe that she was meant to lead them. They named her White Woman because of her clothing.

Hannah's manner of telling this amazing tale and others was as different from Flora Driving Hawk's as the two women were in appearance and character. Flora was short and dark; Hannah was tall, and her coloring reflected her mixed blood. Flora had one living offspring, and she doted on my brother and me, her only grandchildren, whereas Hannah had seven children and, at her death, forty-one grandchildren and 125 great-grandchildren. She permitted us to kiss her cheek, but I don't recall her ever kissing us back. To my child's view, she was incredibly ancient (she was in her seventies when she lived in Okreek), and my kiss barely touched her cheek, for I feared I would damage her delicate skin, which was taut over high cheekbones. I remember feeling a bit frightened of this stern elder, who rigidly held to her devout Congregationalism. As a college student, I discovered that the word *puritanical* described Hannah's moral code.

I sat at her feet trying to do neat and tidy stitches on my sampler (or she'd make me rip them out and start over) and learned patience as I waited for her to continue White Woman's story. Unlike Flora Driving Hawk's richly detailed and dramatically narrated stories, Hannah's were more of a recitation of facts, quickly giving information so that I had no time to ask questions even if I had dared to interrupt. Although both women were educated in Christian boarding schools, Hannah had been trained as an adult to be a missionary and had a longer period of education than Flora had. Hannah's vocabulary and syntax were like that of her white missionary teachers. White Woman's story did not end with her becoming a Ponca leader but continued into romance.

> One day White Woman heard a moan coming from some bushes near the river. She looked and found a man, but one like she'd never seen before. His skin was pale, and his head and face were covered with shaggy reddish hair. It was a white man, ill and near to death. White Woman tended the sick man through a long period of convalescence, during which they fell in love. They learned to talk to each other, and he said his name was MacDonald.
>
> Because White Woman had been captured before she was of age for the Maiden's Ceremony, she took part in one now held for girls of marriageable age, who were to have remained virgin

until they wed. The young men were asked if any of them had known any of the girls as a wife. MacDonald stepped forward and admitted to knowing White Woman in an intimate way. The people did not punish White Woman, nor was she shamed for her lack of chastity. To them, it was fitting that this woman, who had miraculously reappeared, should take this man, who had suddenly and mysteriously come among them.

Later, when I was in college, I interviewed Hannah for a term paper I had to write for a history course and checked to see whether my memory of her stories was correct. I wanted to know more of White Woman and asked what the role of a female chief might have been, but Hannah did not know. I sensed that, as a devout Christian, she was embarrassed, perhaps even shamed, by the un-Christian marriages of our Ponca and Santee ancestors. Because of the sparseness of the oral information about these forebears, I had to search for further details in written history and make some inferences about their lifestyles.

The Poncas are of Sioux stock and related to the Omaha, Osage, Kansa, and Quapaw tribes. Tradition relates that the Poncas separated from the Omahas on the Missouri River and lived near the Pipestone Quarries in present-day Minnesota until driven out by the Sioux to the area that is now Lake Andes, South Dakota. They later settled near the confluence of the Niobrara and Missouri Rivers on the Nebraska–South Dakota border. There fur traders like Mac-Donald encountered them.

Ponca women were apparently accorded high status, for a men's society, Hel'ocka, had its origin in a woman's dream. When she was a little girl, White Woman's father honored her by having tattooing and ear-piercing ceremonies, after which he gave away horses and other gifts. White Woman and other girls so honored by their fathers were the only ones permitted to wear special soft-soled moccasins and were the social elite of the tribe. In addition to being chief, White Woman may have belonged to a society of warrior women who danced with the men before and after battles.

In 1804, the Poncas, always a small tribe, had eighty warriors, but over half were killed in a Brulé raid, and sixty men, women, and children were taken captive. The captives were later released after their Omaha relatives intervened on their behalf. In his 1851 account of Astoria, Washington Irving reports that, in May 1810, Wilson Price Hunt, leading a party overland from St. Louis to Astoria on the

Northwest coast, visited a friendly Ponca village about four miles south of the mouth of the Niobrara. The Poncas warned Hunt to be wary of the Sioux, who frequently raided the Poncas.

It was in this period that White Woman bore MacDonald a daughter, who as an adult was known as Shots through the Breast. Family lore says that she may have received the name after being thus wounded. She, like her mother, married a white man, and she and her husband, Charles LeClaire, had a daughter named Lucille. This child may have been among the Ponca children whom the famed Jesuit missionary Father Pierre DeSmet saw when he visited their village in 1848. DeSmet baptized many Ponca children and adults, but there is no record of Shots through the Breast or Lucille among the Ponca converts.

I relished Hannah's tales of the Poncas even in her sparse style. One was a place-name legend she told of Maiden's Leap, on the Missouri River, from which promontory a young woman leaped to her death rather than live without her warrior lover, who had been killed in battle. My Uncle Donald Ross, Hannah's grandson, was inspired to write of Maiden's Leap, but told it as a Santee tale (many such traditional tales often cross tribal boundaries).

> I am old and crumbling.
> My life and beauty disappear with time.
>
> At one time,
> The river you call Missouri
> Splashed against my side.
>
> I was a landmark for travelers.
> Jean Munier and Lewis and Clark
> Passed by me.
>
> Many peoples have lived around me.
> I've seen them come and go.
>
> Of all,
> I remember Winona and Chaske
>
> Winona was a beautiful child,
> A lovely young woman.
> She ran with the wind and
> Enjoyed the raindrops on her face.
>
> She sat with me many times.
> I knew her secrets, her desires, and
> of her love.

Chaske was her love.
He was a young, brave, daring and
Courageous man.

To him,
Winona was life itself.
She was the hope of his future.

Chaske,
According to the ways of his people,
Chose to be a warrior.
He danced in among the enemy and counted coup.
The people sang of his deeds.

Each time he went with the others,
Winona sat with me,
And prayed for his return.

When they told her that he had died,
She mourned.
She mourned a brave and honored warrior.

She came to me and
Walked to that part
Where the Missouri had broken my sides.

Winona stood and wept.
She looked down my steep sides,
And saw those rough and ugly parts,
She jumped. (Ross 1978, 47–51)

Another legendary account of a woman, the daughter of a chief, who was instrumental in bringing peace between the Omahas and the Poncas, was told by my great-grandmother. Black Bird, chief of the Omahas in the 1790s, was a crafty and cruel leader who ruled with terror. Seemingly with supernatural powers, he would prophesy an opponent's death, and when his foe perished within the allotted time, other enemies were dissuaded from opposing the seer. However, Black Bird had been ensuring the accuracy of his prophecy by slipping arsenic, acquired from white traders, into his enemy's food.

A Ponca band made the mistake of stealing some of Black Bird's horses, and the furious Omaha leader pursued them, vowing to destroy them. The Ponca chief sent four peace emissaries, each carrying a sacred pipe, but Black Bird slew them all. Finally, the beautiful young daughter of the chief offered to be the messenger. Reluctantly, her father agreed, and the girl set off for Black Bird's camp, dressed in her finest and carrying the peace pipe. Her charms persuaded Black Bird to smoke the pipe with the Poncas, and thus there was peace among the people.

The Ponca woman became Black Bird's favorite wife, of whom he was insanely jealous. One of the other wives, who bitterly resented her fall from favor, persuaded a brother to tell Black Bird that the Ponca wife was in love with another. Black Bird flew into a frenzy and stabbed his favored one.

Black Bird's jealous rage immediately turned to bewildered remorse as he stared at the girl lying dead at his feet. He pulled his robe over his head, sat by his dead love, silent and still, without food or water, for three days. He ignored the pleas of his warriors to cease his mourning, and when they tried to remove the corpse, he roared and struck out with his knife.

Finally, a wise man of the tribe brought a baby to Black Bird, lifted the chief's foot, and placed it on the child's neck. This act moved the chief, who stood, weeping, and told the people of his sorrow over his heinous deed. He vowed to keep the peace brought by the Ponca girl.

There is a similarity between this story and that of the western Sioux's White Buffalo Calf Woman, but the pipe-bearing Ponca girl was mortal. There is also some resemblance to the biblical story of Esther, who saved her people. But even though Hannah told Bible stories, she did not tell Esther's. Later, however, when I read the Bible story, I was struck by the similarity of theme, as I was when I encountered Othello. The Moorish king seemed so like the Omaha chief whose name was Black Bird. Esther, her father, Mordecai, and King Xerxes had immortality in the Bible; Othello and his Desdemona gained it through Shakespeare's telling. I was saddened that the tragedy of Black Bird and his Ponca bride was an obscure legend known only to a few tribal storytellers.

Hannah did not know details or dates of the Poncas' history but was proud that they had built homes and farmed on the reservation established in an 1858 treaty. At that time the Poncas ceded their land to the government in exchange for a strip of land six miles wide and twenty miles long on the Niobrara River and Ponca Creek. Under the terms of the treaty the U.S. government promised to safeguard the Poncas' property and lives, but failed to do so. The Poncas, however, kept their promise never to take up arms, despite frequent Sioux raids on their crops and theft of their horses. In March 1865 they were forced to abandon this site and moved to a new reservation twenty miles north of the Santees on the west side of the Missouri River.

By then, Lucille had married, according to Indian custom, her first husband, Pierre Papin, a French trader from St. Louis, by whom she had two daughters. Hannah Frazier's oral genealogy stated that Lucille was later legally married to her second husband, George Washington Howe, born in 1835 in Vermont. The 1880 Dakota census, however, notes the Howes living at Running Water, Dakota Territory, that George was forty-three and his occupation was farmer, and that he was born in Pennsylvania. The same census reports Lucille as age thirty-six, both she and her mother born in Nebraska, and her father born in Canada. Her race was corrected from a B (Breed?) with an M written over, as was that of the children: Mary Ann, sixteen; Elizabeth, thirteen; Hannah, eleven; Edward, eight; Alice, six; Arnold, four; Ida, two; and Ben, one year. White census takers wrote their race as *mulatto* rather than *Indian* since there was no *mixed-breed Indian* designation.

George also operated a trading post at Running Water on what is now the South Dakota side of the Missouri River. Later, the Howes moved to the Nebraska side, where George helped found the town of Niobrara in the area of the Santee reservation.

In the 1970s, I recalled my great-grandmother's history lessons as I did research for *That They May Have Life*, a history of the Episcopal Church in South Dakota. She hadn't told me the dates, but the facts that I read about the Poncas and the Santees were familiar, although related from an entirely different perspective.

In 1870, when William Welsh visited on behalf of the government and the Episcopal Church, the Poncas expressed their confusion over the fact that the government rewarded the preying Sioux but ignored the peaceful Ponca farmers. Antoine, one of the Ponca chiefs, complained about how the Welsh had made friends with the Brulé Sioux who had stolen the Poncas' horses.

Hannah had told of how "the bad Sioux stole the Poncas' crops and horses," and Antoine referred to the continued forays of the Brulé Sioux, who were better armed than the Poncas. In 1872, the government considered moving the tribe to live with their Omaha relatives, but the Ponca chiefs refused. "They had houses and farms, a school, and a church," Hannah said, "and they didn't want to go."

In other words, the Poncas had become peaceful, civilized farmers, which is what the U.S. government wanted of all tribes. By this time the Poncas were even fewer in number—"because the bad Sioux killed so many, and others died of hunger and smallpox," Hannah explained. On a Sunday in the fall of 1876, the faithful Poncas went to church, but did not hear the usual sermon from their minister. Instead, he told them that they were to be moved from their homes and sent far away to live.

"They had to go," Hannah recalled. In 1877, the Poncas were removed to Indian Territory, as present-day Oklahoma was then called. In the 1868 treaty with the Sioux, the Ponca reservation had inadvertently been included in the area reserved for the Sioux. Rather than rescind that decision, the government argued that the Poncas would be better off if removed from the constant harassment of the Sioux.

The journey to Indian Territory was similar to that of the Cherokee Trail of Tears, in that both were forced removals over the Indians' protests. There was no adequate preparation for the move and the needs of the sick and elderly were not considered. Not many adults died on the Poncas' journey, although several children were buried on the way, including Prairie Flower, the daughter of Chief Standing Bear. However, there was widespread sickness and death during the Poncas' first years in Indian Territory.

Among the dead was Standing Bear's oldest son, who, before he died, begged his father to bury him in the Poncas' old burial ground in Nebraska. Standing Bear placed his son's body in an old wagon and found two horses to pull it; then the chief and sixty-six Poncas made the long trek home in the bitter January cold. When the band sought refuge among their relatives on the Omaha reservation, the government ordered their arrest and confinement until they could be shipped back to Indian Territory. Thomas Henry Tibbles, assistant editor of the *Omaha Daily Herald,* heard of the sad plight of the Poncas and took up their cause. Tibbles gave the Poncas' story wide press coverage, which raised a public outcry, first at their removal, and later at the desperate flight of Standing Bear leading his people out of Oklahoma back to Nebraska. Standing Bear, with Tibbles's aid, brought suit against George Crook, brigadier general of the U.S. Army, and, in a historic legal opinion handed down on 12 May 1879, Indians were established as having the same rights as other Americans.

"But our family was all right," Hannah said, telling how her white father, George Howe, protected his wife's family from the tragic turmoil in the Poncas' lives. Indeed, the Howes lived settled, fairly prosperous lives. George was an Episcopalian, and all his and Lucille's children were baptized in that denomination; one son, Edward, became an Episcopal priest. The Civil War had touched them briefly when Uriah Howe, George's brother, came to live with them after deserting the Union Army. The Howes were probably less concerned about the Poncas than about the impact their new neighbors, the Santees, would have on their lives.

Two daughters, Elizabeth and Hannah, married Frazier men, children of Santee exiles who had converted to Christianity while imprisoned in Minnesota in the aftermath of the Minnesota Uprising of 1862. They were transported by boat from Minnesota down the Mississippi and up the Missouri to a barren, harsh reservation at Crow Creek in present-day South Dakota. After three years of privation and hardship, they settled on a reservation at the mouth of the Niobrara River in Nebraska.

"Crow Creek"—Hannah Frazier uttered the name in low, mournful tones as she recalled almost one hundred years later what survivors had told of the place. "It was bad. Horrible. The children got sick on the boat, and they died at Crow Creek. All around in the hills were graves. Your Great-grandpa Charles was a baby there." Then Hannah told of her husband's Santee family, beginning with Charles's great-grandmother.

"Hazzodowin was the sister to chief Red Wing and married James Frazier," she told me as I interviewed her for a term paper for my college course in South Dakota history, but again I had to try to fill in the gaps of her oral narration by consulting written records.

I found nothing written of Hazzodowin, and oral history lacked details about her mother, whose people were the first Sioux encountered by white explorers, fur traders, missionaries, and military men. These first whites to visit the eastern Dakota people made note of their contacts with the tribes, but since the warriors were the ones who greeted them, it was those meetings—white men with Indian men—that were reported.

In the spring of 1660, Pierre Esprit Radisson, the French explorer and fur trader, was visited on Lac Court Oreille, in what is now Wisconsin, by eight Santee men, each with two wives carrying wild rice, corn, and other grains. A few days later, Radisson witnessed the Feast of the Dead when the Dakota people arrived in ceremonial dress, the warriors carrying weapons and leading the procession, followed by the elders (men) and, last, the women loaded with the tepees, which they set up in less than half an hour. The celebration included gift giving and feasting, with wild rice as the main dish, which the women cooked. Radisson's account of this event is the first time that Dakota women appear in written history.

Hazzodowin and her mother could have been among the women accompanying the Dakota men Radisson encountered. However, they would have been thought of as slaves and pawns in male economic transactions by the male, white historians who described Indian women of that period. Their daily tasks would have been viewed as drudgery—as being second class as compared with the warrior-hunter role. Women were reported to attend to all the essential chores while the men "played" at hunting and fishing. Those judgments emerged from the genteel European tradition in which women were idealized and protected from hard physical work and hunting and fishing were recreational rather than subsistence activities.

Hazzodowin would have been appalled had she been exempted from hard work; it was essential to the tribe's survival, as were all Dakota customs, even though the women seemed to have more expected of them than did the men. Hazzodowin was expected to remain chaste until she became a wife early in her teens; then she was expected to remain faithful to her husband. Adultery occasioned the most severe punishment and worst public disgrace for a woman. The husband of an adulterous wife might cut her nose off. This dual standard was true for all Sioux tribes; men were not disfigured for seducing a married woman. One such act caused the separation of the tribe.

Two families were hunting near Lake Traverse, on the border between present-day Minnesota and South Dakota. A young man of one family seduced the wife of one of the warriors of the second family. The wronged husband attempted to get his wife out of the seducer's tepee, but was killed. The victim's father and other relatives went to retrieve his body, but on their way they were ambushed by some friends of the murderer, and three more were killed. The father, who was not hurt, returned to his home village and roused a war party of sixty warriors. The people divided in a blood feud until the murderer and his followers became a separate tribe, the Assiniboine.

As the Dakotas moved west, another band of men also split from the larger tribe, taking many women with them. This group became the Otos and were called *wife stealers.*

During the era of the fur trade among the eastern Sioux, Hazzodowin's tribe was visited by the coureurs de bois, who would be known from Mackinac of the Great Lakes to the Rocky Mountains. These rangers of the woods were itinerant traders who stayed for months among the Indians, adopting their habits and dress and taking Indian wives.

Hazzodowin, my Santee grandmother, would also have known the voyageurs, French men or half-breeds, contemporaries of the coureurs de bois, who traveled by boat or in canoes. They were first employed by the French fur companies and had the same proclivity to adopt Indian ways. Both wandered widely, wherever the fur trade went, and cohabited extensively with Indian women of many tribes.

It was the coureurs de bois and voyageurs with whom the Indians were most familiar, for the licensed officers did not bother with the details of trade with the Indians. These supervisors, sometimes called *factors,* stayed at their company's home base and also cohabited with Indian women. Washington Irving described the French factors as a "kind of commercial patriarch with a self-indulgent rule . . . he had his harem of Indian beauties, and his troop of half-breed children" (1851, 18).

The factor had clerks, Canadians, often mixed breeds, who transported trade goods on the rivers and lakes to the tribes in the winter, the time to trap prime pelts, returning in the spring or summer with the furs they had traded for powder, lead, rum, and tobacco.

Each clerk, who had some education, supervised the uneducated voyageurs, described as "the children of poverty or shame, who from their earliest youth had led a roving life, and who acted as canoe men, hewers of wood, and drawers of water . . . they were a jolly set of fellows in their habits approximating to the savage rather than the European" (Neill 1858, 116). In other words, civilized white men considered them more like the Indians with whom they lived.

At the end of each day, these voyageurs drank and danced to the music of their fiddle-playing compatriots or "purchased the virtue of some Indian maiden, and engaged in debauch" (Neill 1858, 116). When too old to continue in the trade, they retired to Mackinac or some other depot, with an Indian woman to care for them, and their *bois brulé* offspring followed in their footsteps.

Hazzodowin would have assisted in river portages as Indian women did in 1832 on the St. Louis River in Minnesota. Each carried a bag of flour, a trunk, and a soldier's knapsack topped by a baby in a cradle. Indian women were known to carry a keg of one thousand musket ball cartridges as far as a mile without resting, perhaps even wading through the knee-high water of a swamp. It is no wonder the traders wanted an Indian wife, and Hazzodowin became such to the Scotsman James Frazier.

Even though the Santee were polygynous, not every woman wanted to share her husband with another woman. As a child I loved the romantically tragic tales that my grandmothers told, but was shocked by the fate of Anpetusapa, a Dakota woman who did not want to share her husband with another wife.

In the Dakota village at St. Anthony's Falls (now in Minneapolis), Anpetusapa with her toddler son eagerly awaited the return of her husband from a battle. To her dismay, he came to her lodge with another woman whom he had taken as a wife. Anpetusapa was angry and hurt at what she considered to be her husband's rejection. She took their son to a canoe and quickly paddled into the current, which carried it over the falls, plunging mother and son to their deaths.

Although the dreadful act of Anpetusapa (whose name means "Black Day") was not as bloody as Medea's, it was as bitter as any in Greek tragedy. The depths of Anpetusapa's anguish made her act legendary because it was rare for a wife to reject another woman in the lodge—and unthinkably abhorrent for a mother to kill her child.

Hazzodowin and other Santee mothers considered their children their treasure, the precious reason for their being women, and that which ensured the survival of the people. The love of children was paramount among all Sioux tribes. It was not confined to the biological parents, but within the extended family, children were enveloped with tender care and affection. Grandparents, aunts, and uncles gave as much love to children as did their actual parents. Indeed, these relatives were secondary parents who not only gave love but were concerned with the training and discipline of the children. They accepted the children as their own, and although they were aware of the special position accorded the mother and father, the children accepted their status as belonging also to secondary parents. There were no orphans in an extended family. If the biological parents died or abandoned the children, as happened after alcohol use became common, secondary parents assumed the role, and the children continued to be securely cared for and loved.

However, Christian missionaries like Stephen Return Riggs and later-arriving government teachers thought that Dakota children were raised in a detrimentally permissive atmosphere. They considered Santee children undisciplined because even a toddler was allowed to do as she wished, perhaps even suffering burns until she learned for herself that fire was dangerous.

Missionary Riggs did not understand the Santees' child-rearing practices, but he did correctly report that children learned as they played. As a little girl, Hazzodowin played with dolls, sewing for them and learning to decorate their garments with quill- or later beadwork. She played at dressing skins while her mother actually dressed them. In play she learned how to fulfill her adult role as wife and mother.

At the time of first menstrual flow, Hazzodowin and other girls were instructed by older female relatives to be chaste until marriage and after marriage to be faithful to their husbands. Thereafter, until menopause, Hazzodowin would be secluded from all male company for the duration of her monthly flow. This isolation was not punitive; indeed, the time was enjoyed by the women. They had a chance to rest from their labors, to chat and joke with each other, uninterrupted by children or men. The onset of menses meant that a girl was now a woman—able to bear the children who ensured the life of the tribe. This life-giving power was intensified during a woman's flow, so much so that it could hinder a man's skills as a hunter and warrior, hence the isolation.

During her childhood, Hazzodowin's grandparents often relieved her parents by watching over her while her mother was busy at other tasks. In some families, grandparents would even take a child into their home to be raised as their own. Such a child knew and loved his natural parents and was considered to be especially loved by them if they permitted the grandparents to take the child.

In the mother's absence, grandmothers were most likely to assume the mother's role. Charles Eastman, a Santee, recalled how on her deathbed his mother entrusted her infant son to her mother-in-law, and he fondly wrote of the firm tenderness of his grandmother's training (see Eastman 1907a). Eastman's grandmother did not nurse him, but oral history speaks of women long past their childbearing years who put babes to breast and in whom milk miraculously

Table 2: Santee Birth-Order Names

	Male	Female
First	Chaske	Winona
Second	Hepan	Hapan
Third	Hepi	Hapistinna
Fourth	Catan	Wanske
Fifth	Hake	Wehake

flowed. The explorer Zebulon M. Pike noted this phenomenon in the lodge of an Indian he called Chien Blanche, whose old wife suckled an orphaned grandchild. Pike also noted that the child had been sired by an Englishman.

If the grandmother were unable to assume the mothering role, the mother's sisters or the father's brothers willingly took parentless children into their homes. Indeed, these aunts and uncles were called *Mother* and *Father* even if the biological parents lived.

Children each had individual names, as did the adults, since there were no surnames among the tribes. Santee children were given birth-order names that were used in the family in addition to the individual name by which a child was known within the village (see table 2). This was true even after the Santee became Christians. I was baptized Virginia Rose, but to my grandmothers I was Winona, the firstborn daughter. My brother, Edward James, was Chaske, the first-born son.

Thus were my ancestress Hazzodowin and other Santee women reared when the Dakotas were being visited by the coureurs de bois and voyageurs. One of these white men was James Frazier, who accompanied Zebulon Pike on an official U.S. Army reconnaissance of the upper Mississippi in 1805. Pike wrote of his contacts with the Sioux and of the common presence of whiskey among the Dakota tribes.

At Wabasha's village on 10 September, Pike was irate that the chief could not call a council to meet with Pike because most of the people were drunk. However, when James Frazier, who provided interpreters for Pike, suggested that Wabasha's request for alcohol be honored, Pike gave him two gallons of whiskey. Two weeks later, at Little Crow's village, Pike was appalled at the way the traders were dispensing rum on credit to the Indians. He informed the Indians that "their father [the president of the United States] had prohibited the selling of liquors to them. Fraser [Frazier] immediately set the example by separating his spirits from the merchandise in his boats" (Jackson 1966, 1:66). Pike's inconsistency—using alcohol to gain the Indians' cooperation while still enforcing the ban on its sale to them—would be common among later-arriving officials.

The written history of the Minnesota tribes speaks of suicide in connection with Dakota women, reporting that their lives were wretchedly unhappy, full of degradation and drudgery caused by the use of whiskey. In her stories, my Great-grandmother Hannah deplored its use and its effects on the Indians.

One time a woman hid her husband's whiskey because when he drank he turned mean and would beat her and the children. When she would not tell him where she had hid it, the man beat her anyway. The woman was so distressed that she went off and hanged herself in despair. Hannah would shake her head and say, "See how bad whiskey is?"

James Frazier was with Pike when the expedition wintered in Red Wing's village, where according to my family's oral history he "married" Hazzodowin. Little else is known of Hazzodowin; even the origin of her name, "Whistling Woman," has been lost in the oral genealogy. I fruitlessly sought her in written records while doing the research on the Red Wing chiefs for my book *They Led a Nation* (1975b), but I did find an abundance of material about Red Wing, who, according to Hannah Frazier, was Hazzodowin's brother and chief of a Mdewakanton band of the Dakotas.

Pike made no mention of any of the women in Red Wing's village, but he said that Red Wing was "a sensible man" and called him the second war chief in the Sioux nation. Pike also noted in his journal that the chief presented him with a pipe, a pouch, and a buffalo robe (see Jackson 1966, 1:34).

There were several Santee chiefs called Red Wing, so named, oral stories tell, after a family talisman—a swan wing dyed red. The wing was passed down through succeeding generations of male leaders.

The first Red Wing known in written history appeared as early as the Pontiac Wars (1763), when he, a British ally, visited Mackinac Island between Lake Michigan and Lake Huron. Later, this same Red

Wing (now Old Red Wing) again allied himself with the British during the American Revolution, but he remained neutral during the War of 1812. However, a splinter group of Mdewakantons led by Walking Buffalo, Tatankamani, became British allies. By 1817, Old Red Wing's village was at the mouth of the Cannon River, near the site of the present city of Red Wing. Later, after Walking Buffalo became chief, he and his followers rejoined the band at the old village site. Walking Buffalo was the Red Wing whose sister was Hazzodowin. Red Wing, described by Pike as a handsome, intelligent man, respected by all the Santees, was one of the signers of the Treaty of Traverse des Sioux. Under the terms of the treaty, all the Santees' land in what is now Iowa and Minnesota was taken away except for a twenty-mile-wide reservation along the upper Minnesota River.

Hazzodowin, like all Indian women of her time, would have engaged in demanding physical labor and not complained. Even in the cold of winter she would walk as much as ten miles carrying her tepee cover, kettle, ax, child, and maybe even a puppy on her back. In the late afternoon she would stop to make camp and clear away the snow from the spot where she wanted to erect the tepee. Then with her ax she would cut lodge poles about ten feet in length, set them up, and unfold the tepee cover, made of seven or eight buffalo skins. This she drew around the frame and, where the edges met, pinned them together with wooden skewers or tent pins. She then adjusted the poles to make as large a circle as the cover allowed. At the top where the poles crossed, an opening allowed the smoke from the center fire to escape. Buffalo skins, fur side up, served as beds and blankets to warm as many as fifteen inhabitants during the cold night.

Hazzodowin would next cut and haul wood for cooking and warmth and finally prepare supper. If necessary, she could do all this by herself, but when other women were camping at the same place, they helped each other.

There was a strict division of labor in the village, with the men doing the hunting and fishing (although women did both if necessary), the women nearly all the other work. However, in the spring, some of the men assisted the women with the heavy iron kettles that they used after the arrival of the European traders to make sugar once the women had tapped the maple trees. In the fall the men also helped harvest wild rice.

At this time the main source of food for Hazzodowin's people was sturgeon caught in the lake and deer the men hunted in the woods near the home village. Hazzodowin would also have worked with other women to plant corn in the spring at the permanent village, returning in time after the summer's hunt to harvest the crop. Besides doing the planting and harvesting, the women dried corn, squash, berries, and meat, which was stored in bark or rawhide containers (parfleches).

The method that Hazzodowin used to dry corn was to spread the ears on the ground, where they lay until the husks were wilted. Most of the husk was then removed and the individual ears plaited into a long string, which was then hung to dry. After several weeks in the sun and air, the dried kernels were shelled and placed in bark containers. The smaller ears were husked, boiled, then shelled and strewn in a thin layer on a mat or hide and left in the open until the corn was completely dried.

Some of the corn was kept in the lodge, but most of it was stored or cached for later use. Hazzodowin and her female relatives would first dig a hole about eighteen inches in diameter and one to two feet deep. They then scooped out a hollow of five or six feet in diameter and as deep. They lined the bottom and sides with dry grass, then placed one- to two-bushel sacks of corn with grass between the layers. Finally, the cache was covered with more dry grass, up to the bottom of the narrow opening. This was tamped shut with dirt. Corn stored in such a way stayed dry and edible until spring.

After the crops were planted, the fields were left to thrive on their own, and the whole village left for the summer hunt. Hazzodowin's people had no horses—her band of the Santees never fully made the transition to the plains culture before they left Minnesota in the 1860s—so it took them two days of walking to reach the plains where there were buffalo.

I found out how Hazzodowin and her people lived, but I have to imagine how she felt about that life and especially how she felt about being given to a white man. She may have been apprehensive, but have accepted the marriage as her duty. It was not uncommon for an Indian male to offer women to his guests, whether they were Indian or white men who traveled without women. This was a courtesy provided just as food was, but the white traders often responded to the courtesy with prized goods that the tribes did not have. The woman involved in the exchange was at first honored to be so chosen, and her white lover would present her with gifts that she did not have to share with others. But as more and more traders came into the Dakotas' life, such women were no longer held in esteem.

In 1806, perhaps even in Red Wing's village, Zebulon Pike refused a gift of a woman by explaining his faithfulness to his one wife. The Indians who had made the offer replied that he knew of Americans who had half a dozen wives during the winter.

Although James Frazier had a white wife in Canada, he did not refuse Hazzodowin. She bore him a son, Joseph Jack Frazier, whom she treasured as all Sioux women did their children. During the War of 1812, James led or fought with Red Wing's band; then he took Jack, his son by Hazzodowin, to Mackinac. Although he later sent the boy back to Red Wing, James never returned to Red Wing's village himself. Jack, whose Indian name was Ite Maza, Iron Face, was bitter about this: "The only man he wished to kill was his father [because] his father had promised to make him a white man, educate him in a civilized manner," but had not kept his word (Marryat 1941, 29–30).

In his biography of Jack, Henry H. Sibley notes that Jane, Jack's wife, lived in Faribault, Minnesota, where Jack died in 1868 (see Sibley 1950). However, Jack had relationships with several women according to Indian custom, even eloping with and then leaving one nameless girl for the daughter of Grey Iron, with whom he lived for two years. Although Jack apparently did not identify these women to Sibley, the biographer does say that Jack's mother, Hazzodowin, aided them. Only from my family's oral history is it known that one of Jack's wives was called Winona and that she was my great-great-great-grandmother. According to written records, Jack witnessed the killing of Andrew Meyrick, which marked the beginning of the 1862 Minnesota Uprising, and then fled to Fort Ridgely, abandoning his Indian family. The fate of Winona is not known, but her son John's family would be among the Santees exiled for their rebellion born of desperation.

Margaret "Maggie" Frazier.

John Frazier.

Lucille LeClaire Howe.

George Washington Howe.

Santee Normal Training School, about 1894. Second row, second and third from left, Harriet Frazier and Mary Frazier.

Hannah and Charles Frazier at Ponca Creek.

Ponca Creek Congregational Church.

Mary Dubray Ross with daughter Louise.

The Ross home, Okreek, South Dakota.

Winyan Omniciye, Okreek. Left to right: Rachel Roubideaux,
Lucy Little Money, Emma Wright, Nancy Lambert, Harriet Ross.

Harriet Frazier Ross at Milboro.

Edward and Harriet Ross,
fiftieth wedding
anniversary.

SANTEE

We are a desperate people, but we still retain the pride of the Sioux.
We'll not let ourselves be treated worse than dogs in a time of famine.
We fight! We kill the treacherous whites who took our land with only
lies in payment! We burn the homes of the settlers who have spread
like lice on our land. We are at war!

So spoke a Santee warrior in my novel *Betrayed* (1972a), in telling
why his people began the Minnesota Uprising of 1862. The sudden
brutal outbreak shocked the nation, for the Santees had been exposed
to Christianity and civilization longer than the other Sioux tribes. But
living like the white man and adopting his religion had not enriched
the Santees; instead, they endured years of humiliating poverty.

Under the terms of the 1851 Traverse des Sioux Treaty, the Santees
were guaranteed $200,000 for the ceding of their lands. After the
chiefs signed the treaty at one table they were quickly ushered to a
second, at which they were told to put their marks on a second paper.
The Santee leaders believed that they were signing two copies of one
treaty, but in actuality they were signing the "traders' paper." This
permitted the traders to deduct tribal debts from the treaty funds
before the Santees saw the money. Knowing that the Santees were
coming into money, the traders had liberally extended credit, then
multiplied the debt.

The Santees filed a protest with Minnesota's Governor Ramsey, who assured the Indians that the money would be paid according to the treaty. But Ramsey had already disbursed some of the money to the traders and would not give any to the Santees until they signed a receipt showing that they had received the full amount.

After the new Republican administration came into power in 1861, Clark W. Thompson was appointed superintendent of the Minnesota agencies. He visited the Upper and Lower Agencies in July to supervise annuity payments and listened to Santee grievances. He promised that all the past wrongs would be righted and further annuity payment made in the fall. The Santees believed Thompson and as fall neared went to the agencies to await the promised bounty. When it came, it amounted to only $2.50 per head.

A hungry year passed, and discontent flourished in Santee hearts.

"They were starving in Minnesota," is how Hannah began her story of the Uprising, a sad, bitter tale told from the point of view of the Santee, not found in the history books I studied in college.

The Santees had heard that the U.S. Army was weak and doing poorly in its war with the South. Not only had the Santees lost faith in the word of the United States, but now they had no respect for or fear of its armed strength. It seemed the right time to rise up against the only representatives of the United States that they knew—the white settlers of the Minnesota valley. It was a futile war. The desperate Santees went to their western relatives for help, but the Tetons did not believe the warning: "Count on your fingers all the day long and the whites will come faster than you can count. They have pushed us out of our lake lands into the little space of the Minnesota Valley. As they have moved into our country, we have learned too well that the whites show no mercy for our women and children. You will see, some day the whites will covet this land of yours, and then you will learn of their treachery" (Sneve 1972a, 24).

The displacement of a people and the ending of a way of life began on 16 February 1863, when the U.S. government abrogated all treaties with the Sioux of Minnesota and gave their annuity payments to white families of those who were killed during the Uprising. Minnesota never wanted a Sioux Indian within its borders again.

John Frazier's wives, Maggie and her sister-wife, Jennie, were imprisoned with the women and children and old men at Fort Snelling. John Frazier was held with other warrior-aged Santee men at Mankato along with Maggie's brother, Ehamani, who was one of those sentenced to hang but pardoned by President Lincoln. Wacouta and other principal chiefs had been opposed to the war, but they had no control over their young men, many of whom did fight. However, there was no discrimination between innocent and guilty parties as the Sioux were rounded up and imprisoned. On 4 September 1862, the *St. Paul Pioneer and Democrat* reported that Minnesota citizens demanded swift, sure, and terrible Santee extermination. However, only thirty-eight Santee men were hanged at New Ulm; the rest of the Santees were to be deported.

The Santees were now economically, emotionally, and spiritually destitute and, in their helpless misery, turned to the Christian missionaries.

Missionaries had been known to the Santees since Father Hennepin's visit in 1680, but the first organized Protestant effort came with the brothers Samuel W. and Gideon H. Pond in 1833. The American Board of Missions then sent Thomas S. Williamson, missionary and physician, and Jedediah D. Stevens in 1835, accompanied by their wives, teachers Sarah Poage and Lucy Stevens, and a farmer, Alex Huggins, who was to train the Indians in agriculture. In 1837, Stephen Return Riggs and his wife, Mary, joined the Minnesota missionaries, but at first they had little success among the Santees, finding only the mixed bloods and women receptive to conversion:

> There were no obstacles in the way of the women. If a woman changed her religion and her gods, no one cared very much. It was "only a woman." The woman works already. It will not damage her to keep her house, and her person, and her children neater than when she was a pagan. There seemed to be no absolute necessity that she should change the fashion of her dress. It was not unseemly. Rather was it convenient and economical. So that if she kept herself from idols and fornication, she did well. (Riggs 1869, 176–77)

However, when a man converted, much more was required of him. He could have only one wife, he must cut his hair, wear pants rather than a breechcloth (and little else), and go to work.

Santee men resisted, and Riggs reported that, in the years 1842–48, Dakota warriors physically stopped converts from attending church and so frightened the children that they would not go to school. Male converts also died sudden, mysterious deaths, which the unconverted blamed on Christian magic.

Later-arriving Episcopal missionaries met with similar difficulties when their work began in 1859 with the appointment of Henry Whipple as bishop of Minnesota. Whipple sent Samuel Hinman to establish a mission at Redwood.

All the Protestant missionary efforts in Minnesota were disrupted by the 1862 Uprising. Many of the Christian Santees saved white missionaries and settlers, but all were considered equally guilty of the white settlers' deaths. Minnesotans harshly criticized the Christian influence among the Santees, implying that it had been wasted effort. Riggs responded, "Christianity did not prevent the 1862 Uprising; neither did it prevent the Southern rebellion" (1880, 322).

The missionaries followed the Santees to Fort Snelling and Mankato, opening schools for the children and adults and baptizing hundreds before the Indians were deported.

The Santees were assigned a new reservation in Dakota Territory, near Crow Creek on the Missouri River. The journey to this new home began at Fort Snelling, where Wacouta's band made up the largest number of captives. The women, children, and old men were herded onto steamers and shipped down the Mississippi, like loads of cattle, to St. Joseph, Missouri. There they were crowded onto a smaller craft, the *Florence*, on which they were forced to sleep in shifts because there was not enough room for all to lie down. These destitute passengers, voyaging down the waterways where the whites had first found them, probably did not know that the Civil War raging in the South was being waged over the slavery of black men and women who had come to this country packed into ships the same way the Indians were now crammed into riverboats carrying them to alien lands.

In May 1863, in Yankton, Dakota Territory, it was noted that three thousand Minnesota Indians were to be moved to Crow Creek, and on the tenth the steamship *Isabella* passed Yankton with freight en route to Crow Creek. The citizens of Yankton demanded that troops be sent to reinforce those stationed on the Missouri and James Rivers and at Sioux Falls on the Big Sioux. These citizens had nothing to fear, for the Santees' spirits had been thoroughly crushed.

Following the *Isabella*, the *Florence* passed Yankton, "laden with 1,300 Santee squaws and papooses, whose yellow pates stuck from every crack and crevice on the steamboat, from hold to hurricane deck, and gave the boat very much the appearance of a floating haystack alive with redheaded woodpeckers" (Armstrong 1901, 121).

"*Crow Creek*"—Hannah Frazier, her stern composure broken by the sad tale, almost wept one hundred years later as she recalled stories of the horrible conditions the prisoners experienced. "They starved when they got there. The people suffered because there had been no rain and everything was dry. To make it even worse, there were bad Indians who lived in that area, and they didn't want the Santee taking over their home."

The "bad" Indians were the Yanktonai branch of the Sioux tribes, who called themselves the "Middle People" because they lived between the Santee and the western tribes of the Teton. It was this tribe that bore the brunt of the military retribution that followed the Santee Uprising in Minnesota. General Alfred Sully pursued the Yanktonai and bands of Tetons still living east of the Missouri River, destroying their lodges and food supplies and killing warriors fighting to protect the retreat of their women and children. Battling heroically with bows and arrows and shotguns against modern rifles and artillery, the Indians were bewildered and angry at the invading army's ferocious vengeance. Whatever trust they might once have had in the whites was forever destroyed, and they truly became hostile, as designated by historians, and would fight until it all ended at Wounded Knee on 29 December 1890.

Unwanted by the citizens and Indians of Dakota Territory, the Santees, along with the Winnebagos, who were also evicted from Minnesota and Iowa as the result of the Uprising, survived the miserable conditions at Crow Creek, one of the worst situations ever inflicted on prisoners in the United States: "It was a horrible region, filled with the petrified remains of the huge lizards and creeping things of the first days of time. The soil is miserable; rain rarely ever visits it. The game is scarce, and the alkaline waters of the streams and springs are almost certain death" (Heard 1863, 295).

By the time the Santees arrived it was too late to plant crops, which, in the arid land of Crow Creek, would not have produced enough to feed them. The government had to feed them, which was difficult because of the distance from the source of supply. However, the white farmers of the settled part of the territory profited: "Corn is selling at eighty cents and potatoes at $1.50 per bushel to feed our new Indians upon, and so long as their appetites are good so long will prices be better" (Armstrong 1901, 123). Local produce was also sold to the army to feed troop reinforcements at Fort Randall.

Because there were few able-bodied men at Crow Creek, Maggie and other young women labored so that their children and older relatives would survive. They cut and hauled wood to the sawmills, to the boatyard to feed the boilers of the steamships, and to the stoves of the white settlers in the area. They dug the trenches for the army and root cellars for the farmers, for whom they also planted and harvested corn. They cooked and cleaned in the soldiers' mess, did their laundry, and prostituted themselves to earn more money to feed their families.

Despite the hardships, Maggie, who had given birth to a son, Charles, on the way to Dakota, survived. The Crow Creek reservation was abandoned, and the Santees, traveling overland, were moved to the mouth of the Niobrara River in Nebraska, where they were reunited with their men. It was a bittersweet reunion, for now many of the women found out that their spouses had died in prison at Mankato. Others discovered that they no longer had a husband because a newly Christianized man could have only one wife. In the next four months there were fifty weddings at Niobrara at a settlement situated among hostile white settlers whose lands had been appropriated by the government for the new reservation.

"They were starving in Minnesota," is how Hannah Howe Frazier began her story of the 1862 Uprising, and I remembered this when I wrote *Betrayed*. The story began in Minnesota and ended in Dakota Territory, just as the Frazier chronicle did, and I told my story from the Santees' and Tetons' view of their relationships with the whites. Yet my mixed-blood heritage led me to include as well the non-Indian point of view, a dilemma I've faced not only in my writing but in all my life. Walking the path between two cultures has given me perspective on both ways, which can be confusing, as I wrote in a short story, "Grandpa Was a Cowboy and an Indian":

> First I thought I'd stay out of it, but after fists started flying, I jumped in. The first guy that swung at me was a white man so I hit back and was helping the Indians. I thumped away at my white friends till in the confusion an Indian got me in the gut. Now that made me mad. Here I was on his side and he slugged me. I gave him a good one back and then I was fighting Indians. I ended up getting whopped good by both sides and never did make up my mind which bunch I belonged with. (Sneve 1977a/ 1982, 101)

As Great-grandmother Hannah continued her story, I was angered at how the Indians were forced into becoming pseudowhites, yet I sadly understood why the whites thought it necessary that this happen. The missionaries acted from the belief that the Indians were a dying race and that their only salvation was Christianity and white civilization.

Christianity did fill a need in a time when the old way of life was denied the Indians. Ella Deloria, whose father was one of the first native Episcopalian priests, explained this desperate need: "And what good was it now anyway, in pieces? The sun dance—without its sacrificial core: festive war dances—without fresh war deeds to celebrate; the Hunka rite of blessing little children—without the tender Ring of Relatives to give it meaning—who would want such empty leavings?" (1988a, 98–99).

The Indian women more easily made the conversion to Christianity than did the men. Their role as wife and mother had not changed from pre-Christian times, when religion was an integral element of daily life. However, some of white civilization's mores imposed on the Indians through Christianity further lowered the status of Indian women. The following resolutions of the Episcopal Church were passed in 1870, but enforced prior to that date by all denominations working among the Indians:

5. That the Indian custom of regarding the daughter as belonging to the mother, even after marriage, is destructive of the authority of the husband, and the cause of so much trouble as to almost render Christian marriage impossible among the Indians. . . .

6. That the Christian teaching that the husband is the head of the wife should be enforced; and that for the prevention of troubles, young married people should be encouraged, as far as possible, to live in their own homes and not in the families of their parents. . . .

10. That the Dakota custom of making betrothals without the consent of both parties concerned, is wrong; and that none such should be married by the Clergy of the Mission without diligent inquiry and examination, as to whether the parties are to be so united by their own free will, and by their own desire. . . .

14. That as polygamy is forbidden by the law of Christ, that therefore when any Indian having more than one wife is an applicant for Baptism in the Christian Church, he must first choose the one whom he takes for his wife and be joined to her in holy matrimony.

And at the same time it is the sense of this Convocation that he should as far as he is able continue to support the woman put away, and her children, if she have any, so long as she shall live, unless she shall become the wife of some other man. (quoted in Sneve 1977b, 74, 75)

Indian women who were set aside became known as *put aways*, and Maggie became a put away as she and her children were set aside by John Frazier, who had become a Christian while in prison. John then legally married his second wife, Jennie, and with her and their children returned to Minnesota.

In the 1868 treaty with the western Sioux, Samuel Hinman acted as an advocate for his Santees, and article 6 was inserted, which allowed the Santees to remain permanently in their new homes, to acquire title to farms, and to be made citizens in three years. This was a relief to people who had been displaced from Minnesota and then Crow Creek. They built houses and began to farm.

Maggie and her children, Star, Mary, and Charles, remained at Santee, and in 1869, seven months after John left this family, Maggie gave birth to Jessie, her second daughter. Maggie's brother, Artemus Ehamani Frazier (Ehamani took his brother-in-law's surname), took his sister and her children into his home, and Maggie found employment as a laundress at the Santee mission. Artemus was one of the first Dakota to enter the ministry at Santee, and there's no doubt that this helped Maggie get the job, which paid about $5.00 a week.

When Jessie was six years old, she was enrolled at the Santee school, where she studied for the next six years, save for vacation times, when she stayed with her mother. In 1885, Maggie was living with Charles on his new allotment near Center, Nebraska, and Jessie came there for her summer vacation. One evening she became severely ill with symptoms that suggest appendicitis. Jessie's condition worsened during the night, so the next morning Charles and Maggie started with the sick girl to the agency doctor. But Jessie's pain turned to agony with every jolt of the wagon, and they had to stop about halfway to the agency, whereupon Jessie was carried to the house of a friend. Charles went on alone to fetch the doctor, but while he was gone, Jessie died.

Jessie's death surely devastated Maggie, as it would any mother, but even though she was a Christian convert, the feelings for her children came from tribal belief.

Missionary Mary Riggs, whom Maggie knew, was impressed by a

Dakota mother's feeling for her child and wrote a paraphrase of a bereaved mother's lament at the death of a daughter:

Me choonkshe! Me choonkshe! [my daughter, my daughter,] alas! alas! My hope, my comfort has departed, my heart is very sad. My joy is turned into sorrow, and my song into wailing. Shall I never behold thy sunny smile? Shall I never more hear the music of thy voice? The Great Spirit has entered my lodge in anger, and taken thee from me, my first born and only child. I am comfortless and must wail out my grief. The pale faces repress their sorrow, but we children of nature must give vent to ours or die. *Me choonkshe! Me choonkshe!* light of my eyes is extinguished; all, all is dark. I have cast from me all comfortable clothing, and robed myself in comfortless skins, for no clothing, no fire, can warm thee, my daughter. Unwashed and uncombed, I will mourn for thee, whose long locks I can never more braid; and whose cheeks I can never again tinge with vermillion. I will cut off my dishevelled hair, for my grief is great, *Me choonkshe! Me choonkshe!* How can I survive thee? How can I be happy, and you a homeless wanderer to the spirit land? How can I eat if you are hungry? I will go to the grave with food for your spirit. Your bowl and spoon are placed in your coffin for use on the journey. The feast for your playmates has been made at the place of interment. Knowest thou of their presence? *Me choonkshe! Me choonkshe!*

When spring returns, the choicest of ducks shall be your portion. Sugar and berries also shall be placed near your grave. Neither grass nor flowers shall be allowed to grow thereon. Affection for thee will keep the little mound desolate, like the heart from which thou art torn. My daughter, I come, I come. I bring you parched corn. Oh, how long will you sleep? The wintry winds wail your requiem. The cold earth is your bed, and the colder snow thy covering. I will lie down by thy side. I will sleep once more with you. If no one discovers me, I shall soon be as cold as thou art, and together we will sleep that long, long sleep from which I cannot wake thee. *Me choonkshe! Me choonkshe!* (Riggs 1869, 33–35)

No date is noted for the death of the child, nor the location, nor the name of mother or child. The paraphrase is in King James English, and Mrs. Riggs probably used poetic license in rewriting the translation into English. The reference to the coffin could mean that the mother and child were Christian and that burial was in a cemetery; however, missionaries like the Riggses would not have permitted the wailing song or the placement of food in the coffin. Another explanation might be that *coffin* was used in the paraphrase to simplify the poetic wording. The Dakota did not bury their dead in coffins until forced to do so by white custom; however, Jessie and her family were Christian, and the mission provided her coffin. Maggie probably did place food and Jessie's personal belongings with the girl's body, which was wrapped in a blanket.

Like other women, Maggie wept copiously in her grief, wailing and keening in a heart-wrenching, shrill tremolo. Maggie and other early Christian converts did not understand the whites' stoic reserve when mourning the loss of the dearest loved one. One convert advised the whites, "Cry it out. Even a goose when its companion is shot, lies around the place and makes a great outcry. A deer also, when alone in the world, cries out for the lost ones. In like manner, we, children of nature, wail out our sorrow when our friends die. But it is not so with white people; they mourn in secret" (Riggs 1869, 211–12).

Scaffold burial was practiced by both eastern and western tribes, with the corpse dressed in its best clothes. Mourners blackened their faces and slashed their legs. In 1805, Zebulon Pike noted a scaffold burial of two Sioux women, wives of French men, along with one of their children and another relative, all wrapped in new blankets. After nature had reduced a body to bones, it was removed from the scaffold and interred in the earth, if the family were able to return to the site to so do. Thus, it was possible that the mother in the lament quoted above would return in the spring, rebury her daughter, and place choice bits of food on the grave. The feast for the playmates of the child would probably be accompanied with the "giving away" of the dead girl's belongings. It was also probable that the bereaved mother would lie down by the grave and die from exposure or starvation.

Maggie lived on after Jessie's death, alternating for periods of time among her three surviving children. Blind the last ten years of her life, she was residing in the home of her son Star when she took ill. Her daughter, Mary Kitto, took Maggie to her home, where she died two months later. The three children agreed to split the expenses: Charles paid for the funeral; Star paid for the tombstone; and Mary settled some old accounts at one of the trade stores at the agency.

I've often wondered how Maggie had been able to stand the trauma of being set aside by her husband. How degrading it must have been for her, and how hurt and angry she undoubtedly was. Yet she was one of the fortunate ones of like circumstance in that she had a brother who took her in and, later, adult children who cared for her. Other "put-away" wives, unwilling victims of Christianity, did not fare as well.

Prior to the introduction of Christianity, single women, other than widowed grandmothers, were a rarity in Santee and other tribal societies. Now, on the reservation, single put-away mothers often had to struggle to raise their children if there were not a brother or some other relative to give them a home. In the old way, there were no widows or orphaned children because the dead husband's brother often took the widow as his wife and her children as his own.

The Santee had willingly become farmers in their new homes, and many, like Charles and Star Frazier, succeeded. However, many more barely eked out an existence, remaining dependent on government rations to survive. Single put-away mothers and their children were too often a burden that these new farmers could not support. Nor was there room in single-family cabins, and the days of providing a tepee as the family grew were no more.

There had always been more men than women in the warrior societies of the Dakota and their western kin, the Lakota, but the practice of polygamy ensured that all women could marry and have children. Nor was prostitution found in those societies, until the arrival of the white men and their whiskey.

Now, at Santee (and later on western reservations), there still weren't enough men to go around, and the unmarried women and put-away wives came to be considered in the same light as white society viewed unwed women—as objects of pity and scorn. Some of these women resorted to prostitution, which was encouraged by the proximity of soldiers stationed at Fort Randall.

In 1873, one such woman returned ill from the fort and was taken to the agency doctor, who said she had syphilis. Some days later, the doctor realized that the woman had brought smallpox to Santee. An epidemic ensued in which seventy-four of one thousand Santees died. In an attempt to fight the disease, the missionaries isolated the infected and arranged for a doctor from Yankton to vaccinate the Indians. Having experienced the ravages of previous smallpox epidemics, the frightened Santees reacted as Europeans did to the plague, placing the ill outdoors to die or abandoning them in new houses while they pitched tents along streams away from the dying.

The Fraziers were grateful that the epidemic had not taken any of theirs and truly believed that God had spared them to do his work. That first generation of Fraziers on a reservation took willingly to Christianity and were among the first to welcome missionary Alfred Riggs and his family to Santee. In his journal, Charles Frazier recalled that day in June 1870: "The people heard the horn blowing from the steam boat and were very excited, saying, 'It must be Zitkandan Waste (Good Bird) coming.' Older brother (Cinye) Star Frazier met them in a lumber wagon pulled by oxen. The people met them and welcomed them by shaking their hands" (see Frazier 1931).

The Frazier men willingly learned to farm, and they prospered despite drought and a plague of grasshoppers that descended on their farms to strip the cornstalks bare. The Santees were allotted 160 acres of land per adult and sixty acres per child in 1885, and Charles built a house on his and married Hannah Howe on 21 February 1887. Hannah had been allotted land near the Ponca Agency on which Charles also built, and after a third parcel of land was acquired near the Missouri, he erected another house. Charles had learned carpentry at the Santee Normal and is credited with building many houses at the agency in addition to his own.

The Fraziers' and other Santee children were educated at the mission school, which in 1881 became the Santee Normal Training School. The school's purpose was to be an institution for training teachers for the Sioux and other tribes.

Alfred Riggs, the first director of the school operating under the American Board of Missions, believed that the Indians would best learn if they first learned to read and write in their own language. Having so recently suffered the trauma of dislocation, these Santee students were spared the stress of later Indian education policies, which forbade the use of native languages in schools. Nor were they far removed from their homes on the small reservation, and, like Jessie, they were permitted to spend summers with their families.

Santee students who learned to read and write in Dakota were, for all their lives, proud of this ability. Even though they could correspond in English, their letters were always written in Dakota. Charles Frazier wrote his memoirs in his native language, and much of this Frazier chronicle is taken from his work.

Both Charles and Hannah were fluent in Dakota and English, and

Hannah also spoke Ponca. Hannah left no written records, and although her telling of Santee and Ponca life was sparse in detail, it was rich in expression and style because she had been well taught in the use of the English language.

Hannah and Charles lived alternately in their three homes, raising six children, who also attended the Santee Normal (as did several of their grandchildren). Along with other young mothers, Hannah took part in prayer meetings and Winyan Omniciye, the women's society, organized by the missionaries. This was a sewing society, formed along the lines of similar groups founded at the Yankton Mission across the river. The society's purpose was to raise money for their own people, the native missionaries, being trained at Santee. Members made and donated moccasins and other traditional craftwork, which, along with newly learned crafts, were readily sold. Mary Riggs described the women's work: "The women were skilful in cutting designs of flowers, birds and butterflies from bright colored calicos, and hemming them daintily onto unbleached muslin for table covers and quilts. They were very fond of patch work, and even crazy patchwork soon found its way into the homes of Indian women" (1928, 50).

Thus, in the nineteenth century Santee women learned to make quilts, a craft that would become an art form among Sioux women in the twentieth. The Santee women liked the crazy patchwork, but later, among the Lakota, the star quilt was favored because of its resemblance to the traditional, geometric quill design of the morning star, a symbol of a new day and new life.

The sewing society met every Wednesday at Santee, as Mary Riggs recalled:

> The women appeared with their babies, at the Dakota Home [the girls' building at the school], soon after dinner. The great bundle of work was laid in the middle of the floor, the work was distributed, and in a short time all were chattering and working as busy as bees. The babies had a good time too, crying, laughing, rolling, creeping—they made the meeting a lively place. Then in time to get home before dark, the work was laid away, and after the prayer meeting they hastened homeward. These Dakota women are never weary in well doing. (Riggs 1928, 51)

In the later-established western Christian missions Indian women also formed similar groups. They welcomed these social contacts, which were so like the old days when women of one family helped women of another tan hides or prepare a lodge cover, all the while gossiping, laughing, or weeping—sharing community sorrow and joy.

Hannah was skilled in working with other women, a talent that she would put to wider use in the coming years.

ROSEBUD

By 1901, Charles, thirty-six, and Hannah, thirty-one, with six children, had prospered farming their various allotted lands. They owned three houses with barns, cows, turkeys, chickens, and pigs. It was a good life on the Santee reservation among their relatives. But they gave it all up when Artemus (Ehamani) urged his nephew Charles to enter missionary work. Charles had begun his missionary studies at the Santee Mission early in 1900, finishing the course in October 1901. Hannah supported Charles's new calling and did not dispute his decision to accept a missionary assignment at Salt Camp on the Rosebud, home of the Sicangu, who had raided Ponca villages in the not too distant past.

Hannah and Charles said farewell to their relatives and loaded the six children and what household goods they could into a covered wagon. Hannah did not tell, nor Charles write, of how heart wrenching it must have been to leave the well-ordered security of their lives among family and friends for unknown dangers among the Sicangu, whom the whites still considered a hostile tribe. Thirty years later, in his memoirs, Charles briefly recalled the trip to the Rosebud:

> We started our journey on October 1, 1901. The trails were
> bad and so were the creeks. There was a lot of sand to go through
> since we were in Sand Hill country. This made travelling very
> hard. Each day the horses would be very tired by late afternoon
> and I would stop and rest them and feed them oats. By the time

we reached Todd County the horses were very tired but each day we had to keep going until we reached water. One day, in particular, the horses were so tired and we did not find water until 11:00 P.M. (see Frazier 1931)

After nine days, the Fraziers reached Salt Camp, where they found a small house waiting for them. On the first Sunday, the Sicangu came to look over this Indian minister and his family, but only a few entered the church. Many of the young men never bothered to dismount but sat on their horses and watched, curious and wondering about this Santee man and his Ponca wife who could read and write and lived like the whites.

After three weeks of similar Sunday watches, Hannah cooked a big meal for the observers, who willingly accepted the invitation to eat. As a result, the next Sunday the church was crowded even though Hannah did not have another meal for them. The one effort of sharing and Charles's eloquent words apparently had persuaded the people to attend services regularly.

Hannah held women's meetings similar to those at Santee and assisted Charles with visiting the sick and with Bible studies. But here, in Lakota land, they at first had difficulty understanding the Sicangu tongue and had to learn the nuances of the linguistic variations in the related languages.

On their first Christmas Eve at Salt Camp, disaster struck. A program was to be held in the church, and the people had brought food, which they put in the Fraziers' house. The program had just started when Charles heard, "Fire, fire!"

The minister and the frightened congregation rushed to get out the rear door of the church. Somehow, the small Christmas tree inside the Frazier house had caught fire, and now the whole house was ablaze. Helplessly, Charles, Hannah, and the congregation had to watch the house and all its contents burn to the ground within the hour. Everything was gone except for the clothing the Fraziers wore.

The Fraziers spent a frigid, frightful night in the small church. Hannah, with tears in her eyes, handed the youngest child to Charles while she tried to comfort the others, who were weeping with fright, hunger, and cold. Their thoughts were of Santee, "home where we had three houses and did not have to suffer in any way," Charles recalled.

Miserable and shivering, the children slowly stopped crying as the family comforted and warmed each other, huddling near the stove. In the stillness they heard a man yelling outside the church.

The unknown man was speaking to the Sicangu camped in the churchyard. He told them that the minister had come to help them and that now he and his family needed their help.

The Sicangu and most Indians with a tradition of revering their *wicasa wakan* (holy man) transferred that respect to Christian ministers and priests. They also willingly shared their possessions with others. The Salt Camp congregation, the first adapting to the reservation, were a poor people, but they gave two blankets and a pillow with which the grateful Fraziers made a bed for the children.

The next morning there was snow, and the Fraziers were hungry and cold, as was the congregation, who had stayed the night outside the church. They had done all they could to help the minister and his family, but the loss of food in the fire was a hardship for them, for they probably didn't have much more than what they had brought to share at the Christmas program. Charles held the Christmas morning service, and the people, unable to do more, left.

Hannah worried about her children as a fierce blizzard, so common to prairie winters, raged around the small church building. Their clothing, food, furniture, utensils—all was gone, and now it seemed as if the congregation had abandoned them.

The family huddled together for warmth, and Charles prayed. Later in the morning, when their hope was waning, they again heard a voice call outside the church. Their new congregation had not forgotten them but had sent someone to help. Charles opened the church door to a man from the subagency (probably from Parmalee) who had come to rescue the Fraziers. He loaded the shivering children and their parents into a spring wagon and covered them with blankets for the seven-mile ride through the cold blizzard to the Catholic church. There, the caretaker, Steven Murray and his wife, Rosalie, welcomed the destitute family into their small home.

Unbelievably, it was no stranger who opened her arms to Hannah; Rosalie had been a classmate at Santee, and she now lovingly shared clothing, blankets, and food. Hannah, comforted to find a friend in her calamity, called Rosalie "sister."

Hannah and the children stayed with Rosalie until Charles built a log cabin at the church. A fellow missionary, the Reverend J. F. Cross, brought the material for the cabin and provided replacement clothing, blankets, food, and a cook stove.

The Fraziers were barely recovering from the fire when the horses they had brought from Santee died of a disease afflicting all horses in the area. For two months, before other horses were acquired, the Fraziers were on foot, with Charles walking to visit his congregation and to the agency for supplies.

"But," as Charles wrote, "our sorrows had not ended." In June, their youngest son, two years old, was stricken with an illness and died on 4 September 1903.

Hannah and Charles prayed for strength and courage to accept this great loss. By adopting the white man's religion and lifestyle, great sacrifices were made. So far from home and the loving support of family, they had to endure this bitter loss in the isolation of a strange land. "Going through this all alone was hard," Charles wrote, but if their desolation tested their faith, he did not write of it. Later, Hannah, who never forgot the devastation of this lonely tragedy, instilled in her surviving children a strong sense of family loyalty and responsibility. Hannah's life on the Rosebud was similar to the lives of white pioneer women, who had to adapt to the rigors of nature and loneliness in a new land.

The people of the Salt Camp congregation lived four to five miles away from the church, but three young men came by, perhaps in answer to the Fraziers' prayers, and with their help Charles and Hannah buried their son. Fifty years later, their daughter Harriet Frazier Ross made annual visits to the grave of her youngest brother at Salt Camp.

Hannah reluctantly left the resting place of her youngest child, the first of her children to predecease her, when in 1904 Charles answered a call to serve at Ponca Creek, south of Herrick, South Dakota. There were no longer any Poncas, Hannah's tribe, living there, but the Sicangu Chief Asampi (Milk) and his band had settled and taken allotments along the creek. There the Fraziers lived in a three-room house with a lean-to, and again Hannah ministered to the women and assisted Charles in the mission work. Fifty years later I sat at Hannah's feet and listened to her recollections of Ponca Creek. She did not speak of her daily routine, but of a devastating flood that inundated many of the Indians' homes along the usually placid Ponca Creek. The Fraziers' home was spared, but they were isolated for several days by high water over the only road to their place.

"As the water went down," Hannah told,

there were many fish trapped in pools along the creek. The children caught them with their hands. At first we enjoyed having so much fish to eat, but soon the whole creek bottom reeked of rotting fish. The children came from play covered with mud and stinking of dead fish. I made the children stay away from the creek, but then some of the people came to get Charles. They were excited and alarmed because they'd found a monster in a muddy pond. The children had to go see, so we all went to look.

It was a strange looking fish—about as long as Charles was tall [almost six feet] with an odd long mouth—sort of flat shaped. It was dying in the mud. The people were afraid of it even after it was dead.

As an adult, I accompanied my husband and son on a fishing trip on the Missouri. They were after paddlefish, and when they caught one, I wondered if this were the monster of Hannah's story, which somehow made it from the great river to the flooded Ponca Creek.

Hannah enjoyed the time at Ponca Creek, but uncomplainingly moved to Tripp County in 1909, where Charles helped organize the Congregational Church at Millboro, South Dakota. They bought deeded land in nearby Clearfield and lived there among the whites until 1913.

Hannah found family at her new home on the Keyapaha River, where Elizabeth and Enoch Raymond had settled. Enoch Wheeler Raymond had been the first agent at the Whetstone Agency on the Missouri River in 1868. His wife was Elizabeth Papin, Lucille Howe's daughter and Hannah's half-sister. Later, the Raymonds' son William would marry Julia Menard, an Oglala, and they would have twelve children. One son, Enoch II, married Hannah Frazier's daughter Mary, thus deepening the family relationship.

Also near Millboro, Mary Comes Out, a Brulé, lived on her allotment with her husband, Joseph Ross, Scots trader and freighter. Mary's first husband, Gustavus Butler, had been murdered at Whetstone, and she would outlive not only Joseph, her second spouse, but also Luke Brown and Louis Good Voice, her third and fourth husbands. Mary had two daughters from the first marriage, a son from the second, and another daughter from the third. Her last marriage produced no children.

Mary Comes Out's son, Joseph Ross Jr., first married Susie Smith, by whom he had Jesse, a son. His second wife was Mary "Mollie"

Dubray Rose, who bore Edward (my grandfather), William, Louise, and Nellie.

Mary Dubray, oldest child of six born to Antoine "Chet" Dubray and Louise, his second wife, was thirteen years old when her mother died. She would be raised by her father's other wives, Julia Moran and Jennie Bissionette, and help rear her half-brothers and -sisters.

Like her mother-in-law, Mary Comes Out, Mary Dubray also made several marriages. The first with James Gerue was childless. The second with James Wright produced Jesse, William, and Sarah. Mary had been separated from Wright for some time before Sarah's birth, and the girl went by the surname of Ross. When Sarah died in about 1909, her father, Jim, her only heir, deeded the girl's allotment to Mary Ross in "settlement of any claim she might have for rearing their daughter, Sarah, after they had separated."

These two Marys certainly lived life to its fullest, and I am amazed and awed at their several marriages and widowed states, their numerous pregnancies, birthings, let alone their rearing and burying children. They surely were tough, adaptable ladies with tremendous physical and emotional stamina.

Mary Dubray Wright looked like a white woman but spoke only Lakota and signed with her thumbprint, for she could neither read nor write. She and Joseph Ross Jr. were neighbors of the Enoch Raymonds, with whom Joe freighted. The Ross-Frazier-Raymond family relationships intensified when Mary and Joseph Ross's son Edward married Harriet Frazier, the sister of Mary Raymond.

Edward and Harriet were married by the Reverend Francis Frazier on 15 February 1911 in the Community House at Millboro. They lived on Edward's land allotment until his mother became ill and then moved to her home on the Keyapaha River.

George was Chaske, and Rose, my mother, Winona, of the nine children born to Harriet and Edward. Rose's memories of living at Grandma Mary Ross's home go back to when she was five years old. The Ross family was traveling in a wagon, with George, Rose, and Alma seated in the wagon bed. Rose leaned over the side to watch the ground move under the wheels. Mesmerized by the motion, she lost her balance and fell from the wagon, and its wide rear wheel ran over her leg.

"Rose fell out!" George called, and his father stopped the wagon some distance from where the little girl lay.

"Get back in the wagon," ordered Rose's father, but she could not; her leg was broken. Her father picked her up, put her in the wagon, and drove twenty miles to the doctor in Winner. The little girl's leg was set in a heavy cast, immobilizing her for several months.

When Rose was six, Edward and his brother-in-law Earl Frazier were arrested for bootlegging, selling whiskey to the Indians. Only Ed was convicted, and he was sentenced to one year in the state penitentiary. Rose believes that her father was sentenced because he looked like a white man who could easily buy the liquor, whereas dealers wouldn't sell to Earl because he was definitely an Indian.

"Grandpa Frazier helped us out," Rose recalled. He found a small, one-room house in Winner where Harriet and four of the children lived until Ed's release.

Rose started school in Winner, and her memory of that year was that it was a bleak Christmas in the little house. "For my present, Mom made a dress for my doll because its old gown was ragged and dirty. My own dress was old too and getting short as I grew, but I was happy to have the new doll dress. I was supposed to take something to show and tell about at school, so I took the dress. The only new thing I had."

After Ed's release, the family moved back to Mary Ross's home along the Keyapaha and lived with her until Ed built a house on his allotment across the river. School was within walking distance for George and Rose if they could ford the shallow river in the fall or walk over on the ice in the winter. But when the river ran high in the spring, they had to walk several miles around to cross the bridge.

Harvey and Olive were born here, and after each birth, Harriet was bedridden for long periods of time, during which Rose assumed the household chores and the care of her younger brother and sister. "It seemed like I was always carrying a baby," Rose remembered. "I was skinny, and the easiest way to carry the baby was on my hip."

As an adult, Rose suffered backaches, and a medical exam and X-ray disclosed a curvature of the spine, caused, she believes, "by carrying heavy babies while I was still growing."

In addition to caring for her younger siblings, Rose did the cooking. "Mom would tell me what to do, and expected me to do it right. Most of the time I did, but once I miscounted the number of potatoes I was to cook, and had to go without because it was my mistake."

During the summer the children's playground was the shallow Keyapaha, where they went every afternoon.

I'd put Olive in a place where the water barely touched her toes, then I would play with the others. I'd check on her once in a while, and she was happy sitting there splashing her hands and watching the others.

But one time I looked, and all I could see was Olive's hair floating on top of the water. I screamed and started feeling around in the water. George helped me look and both of us found her under water stuck in the sand. I grabbed her hair to lift her head out of the water, while George dug her out.

The sand had shifted under the baby, sucking her under the water, Rose explained. "We were so scared because she was unconscious. We shook her upside down and pounded on her back until she started to cry. She had sand in her mouth, which we scooped out, but she swallowed a lot of it when we tried to rinse her mouth out. After that she wouldn't sit in the water anymore. We were all so scared, but we never told Mom that her baby had almost drowned."

While the children played at the river, Harriet remained at home, alone in bed. The children were expected to return home before supper. "But one afternoon we were having such a good time, that the sun was setting when we got home. Mom was frantic with worry, and very angry. 'Tell Rose to come here!' she called from the bedroom. I went in. 'Bend over,' she ordered. I did. She took the hairbrush that she kept by her bed to punish us, and spanked me. I was the only one punished. I was the oldest girl and was responsible for all the others."

During this time, Edward was a freighter hauling cream from Millboro to Colome, South Dakota. He also hauled lumber from Millboro to Springview, Nebraska, and other supplies out of Crookston, Nebraska. It was a successful operation, and he owned eight horses and twelve wagons for the business.

He also farmed his mother's land along with his until 1927, when the crops failed and cattle died of disease. Then Ed had to sell the freight wagons and horses. The family moved to "Uncle Sam's" place south of Okreek. Sam Bordeaux, the husband of Ed's half-sister Susie Butler, let them live there for two and a half years.

The family moved from there to Soldier Creek, near Rosebud. "It was a hard time for us. Dad worked at odd jobs, but George, Alma, Jeanette, and I were sent to the Rosebud Boarding School so that the little ones, Harvey, Olive, and Leo [born at Uncle Sam's], could have food to eat at home."

"Oh, how I hated boarding school," Rose recalled.

We spoke only English and knew very little Indian. The other kids spoke Indian at home, but couldn't at school. The bigger girls said we were trying to be "whites," and they really were mean to us; they were always punching us, or pinching, or pulling our hair.

George never said anything, but I know it was worse for him. He wouldn't put up with it, so he fought the boys who picked on him. It was hard, but after a while they left him alone.

Jeanette and Alma were so young and homesick. Whenever they saw me they cried, then I would cry too.

The succeeding years were easier for the Ross children. Rose became one of the big girls, older ones who were given charge of the little girls returning from their summer vacations. "We had to shampoo their heads after they'd been deloused with kerosene. Then we had to use fine-tooth combs to get the nits out. I hated it. We were never lousey at home, Mom made sure of that! But every fall I'd catch lice from those little girls. Then I'd have to kerosene my own head; I was so ashamed."

Other memories Rose had were of the military routine that the staff used to control the students. "We marched everywhere: from the dorm to the classroom, to the dining hall, to church in Mission. Boys and girls were always separated, but that didn't keep them apart," Rose laughed. "I started going with Jimmy."

Ed, Rose's father, came to work at the boarding school first as the dairyman, then a farmer, a policeman, and a night watchman. As each job phased out, he was given another.

His mother, Mary, had built a house at Okreek, where she lived with her daughters until she died. Mary left the property to daughter Rose, who then permitted Ed and his family to move there after she married and moved away.

Edward was often away from home with his freighting and later during the depression years, when he worked at seasonal ranch jobs. Harriet's life was busy caring for their seven children. Her staunch Christian faith, like her parents', sustained her during the trials of the violent deaths of two children: Alma died of burns received when a gas oven exploded, and Leo was brutally murdered—a homicide that was never solved.

After the move to Okreek, Harriet was organist at the Episcopal Calvary Chapel, where she also taught Sunday School and served many terms as president of the Winyan Omniciye. She made quilts with the women to raise funds for the needs of the church and did fine handwork to decorate her home.

Harriet had rallied to her parents' support when tragedy and controversy flared after World War I. Two brothers, Ben and Arthur, enlisted in the army in 1917; Ben returned safely home, but Arthur was reported killed in the Argonne region in 1918. The body that was buried as Arthur Frazier with full military honors at Niobrara on 18 September 1921 was later identified as one Art Lopez.

Arthur Frazier had been taken prisoner by the Germans, but somehow he had escaped and returned to America. Suffering from amnesia, he wandered the country until he was befriended by a woman in Ponca City, Oklahoma, who cared for him because he resembled her brother, who had been killed in the war. She had his picture circulated in various Indian news outlets, and one found its way to Charles and Hannah. They recognized the unknown soldier as Arthur and hurried to Oklahoma. They found Arthur in a mental institution, not knowing who he was or where he was from. At the sight of Hannah, he rushed to embrace her, calling, "Mama," and Hannah was sure he was her son.

Two other Frazier sons, Ben and Earl, were also victims of mysteriously tragic circumstances. Earl was found dead of causes unknown in Sioux City, Iowa, in March 1942, only two years after Ben died. On 14 March 1940, Ben was driving a truck from Mission to Rosebud when a sudden blizzard struck. After the storm, the truck was found, but Ben was missing. A fruitless search was conducted in the area, but given up when no sign was found of the missing man; it seemed that his body would never be found. Ben's brother-in-law, Edward Ross, would not give up, however, and asked a medicine man to do the *Yuwipi* Ceremony, which was meant to find lost people. Edward and his son Harvey attended, and the medicine man told them where to find the missing Ben. The search was resumed following the directions given by the medicine man, and Ben's body was found on 25 April 1940.

I don't recall ever hearing Hannah or Harriet or Flora discuss this tragic episode that is part of the family lore. So I never knew if they recognized the irony of this Christian family turning to a cultural belief that they had forsworn. Later, long after Hannah and Harriet were gone, while doing the research for *That They May Have Life* (1977b), I found incidents of baptized Indians attending church on Sunday morning after participating in a Sweat and Pipe Ceremony the day before or ingesting peyote in the Native American Church and then taking Christian communion. The anomaly of these diverse beliefs apparently caused no conflict in their religious lives.

Hannah Frazier, who had suffered fire and the death of a child without family support, had instilled a strong sense of family responsibility and loyalty in her children. Harriet Ross did the same, and her home at Okreek became the pivotal point in the lives of her adult children, thirty-two grandchildren, and the sixty-six great-grandchildren born before her death. No matter how far the family scattered, the children and grandchildren made frequent visits "home," where Harriet welcomed them warmly.

If I were asked to name "home," it would be the Ross's place in Okreek, where there was always love and security. I could depend on it never to change, to be the stable spot in my life where my parents left my brother and me when they attended summer church meetings or traveled to Sioux Falls for work to supplement Dad's meager salary. Later, it was a haven for Mother, my brother, Edward, and me—homeless after the death of James, my father. I don't remember sorrow in Harriet's house, but I do recall quiet contentment and music.

Harriet, who inherited a beautiful singing voice from her parents, loved music. Often, several generations gathered around her upright piano to sing the gospel hymns she favored. Other times, she accompanied Ed while he fiddled lively "jig" tunes or mournful cowboy songs. How pleased with myself I was when I learned to read music well enough to accompany Harriet's singing and Ed's fiddling.

For her granddaughters, Harriet made buckskin Indian dolls with tiny beaded moccasins and horsetail hair adorned with ribbon and fluffs of feathers. Her daughter Rose traced Harriet's doll pattern and uses it to make dolls for her granddaughters.

Gifted with a psychic sixth sense, Harriet would open her door with, "I knew you were coming because when I got up this morning I decided to make corn bread [or donuts or fry bread]. I thought of you while I made it, because I know it's your favorite."

Harriet believed, as Mary Riggs had noted a hundred years earlier, that "the Dahkotahs assert that a mother is with her absent children whenever they think of her, and that she feels a pain in her breast (or heart) whenever anything of moment happens to them" (Neill 1858, 70).

Harriet ended every day with prayer, and the evening ritual brought serenity and comfort to the most troubled family member who might be present and to the absent ones who reported feeling surrounded by her love.

Once when she was not expected to live and lay close to death in the hospital, she felt herself rise from her body to a lovely light. But she looked down at her body and saw Edward sitting forlornly by her side, and she could not leave him—not yet. After she recovered, she asked him, "How would you get along, if I had died?"

After over sixty years of marriage, Edward seriously considered the question and then answered, "Well, our maid of honor's still alive."

Grandpa Ed had a wry sense of humor, which I did not come to know until I was an adult. My childhood memories are of him tinkering with his car to get it running so that he could be off to whatever seasonal job he had. I remember Grandma being furious with him when he came home tipsy, but that was when he was the most fun.

At those times his fiddling soared and roared with joy. He stomped and jigged, bobbed and swayed, hollered and laughed. "Edward! Edward!" Grandma tried to calm him down, but I saw the smile lurking at the corners of her mouth. The music sweetened, slowed, and he waltzed around her, ending the performance with a smacking kiss on her cheek.

If Ed's occasional binges caused problems in my grandparents' marriage, I didn't know it. All I knew as a child was how much fun Grandpa was when he made the fiddle sing and when this usually taciturn man told how it was to be a cowboy *and* an Indian. He loved to read pulp westerns, and I always took copies to him when I went to visit. One time I gave him a copy of Badger Clark's cowboy poems, which he enjoyed so much that he memorized and recited them.

Grandpa was lonely without Harriet, who died in 1975. In her final illness, before her children were alerted, each one had a sudden sense of Harriet's calling as she had done when they were children. And all went home.

Years after Grandpa died, I wrote a short story and a poem recalling Ed's life (the poem was modeled after Badger Clark's verse).

Grandpa Was a Cowboy and an Indian

Grandpa was a cowboy and an Indian
And he would often be confused,
'Cause he didn't look like either one,
A fact he often mused.

His pa was a white freighter
Who drove mule-pulled wagon trains.
His ma, a Lakota maid,
A nomad of the plains.

Grandpa did a fancy jig
While his fiddle played along,
Or he'd croon the long, sad verses
To old-time cowboy songs.
Still, he sang Lakota chants
Of proud lost warrior days,
Stepped high in bells and moccasins
To the beat of Indian ways.

Grandpa wrangled for white ranchers
From the Keyapaha to the Jim,
'Til he wed a Santee maiden
Then on his allotment, his own spread did begin.
Grandpa raised horses and cattle
That thrived on the prairie grass.
Nine children grew strong and healthy
Working at the ranch's tasks.

He struggled, but never prospered,
Watching the years and children go,
'Til the ranch died with the cattle
And the Keyapaha ceased to flow.

Grandpa was still an Indian
When his cowboy days were done,
Then he rode the range of memories
Of ways forever gone.
Tiyospaye mourned his passing
And the drum beat at his wake,
While gospel hymns were harmonized,
Beseeching God his soul to take.

Grandpa's a cowboy and an Indian
In God's eternal band
Where he'll ride forever
In heaven's prairie land.

Grandpa was buried with his cowboy hat and an eagle feather, and a drum slowly beat as singers chanted a warrior's farewell.

Flora Clairmont, about nineteen years.

Robert and Flora Driving Hawk, about 1923.
Son James is riding the horse.

Robert and Flora Driving Hawk and their Model A Ford on the
Running Water Ferry, 15 August 1948.

Flora Driving Hawk in the author's home, 1969.

Rose Ross and James Driving Hawk, wedding, 26 May 1932.

James Driving Hawk with Eddie and Virginia, Ponca Creek, 1940.

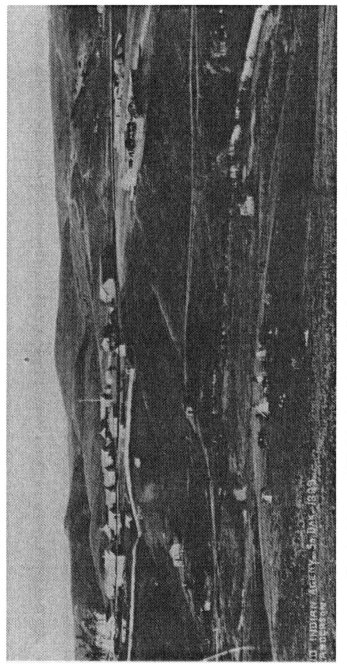

Rosebud Agency, 1889. John A. Anderson Collection, Nebraska State Historical Society.

Ring Thunder Village, Agency District, about 1893. John A. Anderson Collection, Nebraska State Historical Society.

Sioux celebration, 1889. At far right is James Clairmont or Claymore. John A. Anderson Collection, South Dakota State Historical Society.

Rosebud Agency, 1894. Front row, seventh and twelfth from left, High Bear and Ring Thunder. John A. Anderson Collection, Nebraska State Historical Society.

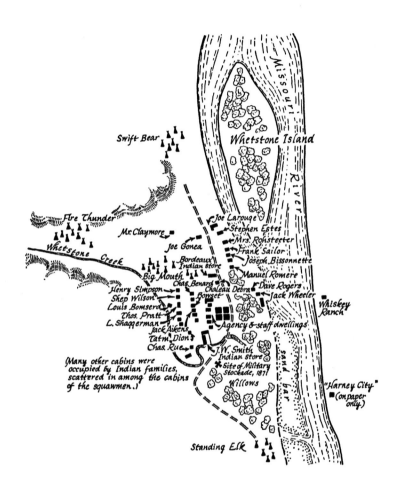

Whetstone Agency 1868–71. From *Spotted Tail's Folk*, by George E. Hyde, based on maps in *Wi-iyohi*, South Dakota Historical Society, vol. 8, no. 2, 1934. Copyright 1961, 1974 by the University of Oklahoma Press.

COMPLETING THE CIRCLE

Rose Ross, my mother, completed the eighth grade at the Rosebud Boarding School, and she joined her brother George at the Santee Normal Training School, where their Frazier grandparents had been among the first pupils, and where the Frazier children had been educated. This move to a place far removed from home, and what to Rose was a strange land, was not as traumatic as the first year at the Rosebud Boarding School had been. She was older, toughened by the harsh life at the Rosebud school, and Rose had another comfort.

"While I was still at the boarding school, I started keeping steady company with Jimmy, your dad," Rose told me sixty years later. James, the only living child of Robert and Flora Driving Hawk, had planned to finish high school at the Haskell Institute in Lawrence, Kansas, "but he followed me to Santee," where they stayed for three years and were married before they graduated.

The wedding, on 26 May 1932, was performed by the Reverend Paul Barbour, an Episcopal priest, a staunch friend of Flora and Robert Driving Hawk's who would become James's mentor.

The elder Driving Hawks built Rose and Jimmy a two-room house next to their own small home in Mission. I was born in February 1933, and that summer and fall Jimmy worked in a WPA camp in Wyoming with his uncle Dick Clairmont. After his return, Jimmy began studying for the Episcopal priesthood under Father Barbour's tutelage.

My brother Edward was born in 1935, and later that year we

moved to Milk's Camp at Ponca Creek, where James had charge of All Saints Episcopal Chapel. The chapel was across the creek from the Congregational church where Hannah and Charles Frazier had lived.

My memories of our stay there are sad and happy, tinged with nostalgia for that short time of being part of a loving family. I was five when I first attended the Milk's Camp Bureau of Indian Affairs Day School. Dad walked me to school and came to get me. We walked along the creek, its smooth running waters reflecting the golden trees. I watched a dry leaf fall into the water and followed it downstream until we cut across a field. In the winter the creek froze solid, and sometimes Dad pushed me on a sled. In the spring we avoided the creek because the low land about it was soggy and muddy. "Stay away from the creek," my brother and I were warned as the placid stream overflowed its banks.

We had a dog, a mixed German shepherd we called "Soup" because one member of the congregation teased us that the dog would make good soup when we ran out of food. My brother Eddie had a toy stuffed red rooster that Soup played with. She'd growl and shake it and then drop it at our feet as a signal to throw it so she could retrieve it. She'd dash off with it, and we'd chase her across the prairie, zigging and zagging, but always ending up at home. Soup was our playmate, for we never saw other children save on Sundays and at school. She was our companion on excursions over the prairies to gather wildflowers or to the creek to float stick and leaf boats. Soup stayed with us, never straying to chase rabbits or squirrels, and she knew when it was time to go home. She nipped at our heels and herded us in the right direction, tugging on our clothes if we dawdled.

It was a good place to be a child, but life was not easy at Ponca Creek. My father kept a diary as part of his pastoral duties, and his terse entries began on 21 January 1936: "2 PM. severe blizzard—work on W.P.A." All the next two years Jimmy was part of an all-male Indian WPA, part of the federal government's national Works Project Administration, which provided jobs to the unemployed. For the next two years Jimmy was part of a repair and painting crew that worked even in the coldest weather. On 3 February he wrote, "W.P.A. Left side of my countenance froze."

Other entries during those years voice his concern that "Rose and the kids will have enough to eat even though we 'fasted from meat' for several weeks." He wrote of riding into Herrick in a parishioner's wagon to get coal to heat the church and our two-room house. When there was no money to buy fuel, he chopped wood along Ponca Creek.

The dog Soup always accompanied him into the woods. On one such expedition the daylight was fading when Soup came home alone. The dog whined and nipped at Mother's heels and tugged at her dress, just as she did when she wanted Eddie and me to go home. Rose was frantic; she knew something had happened to Jimmy. She had to follow the dog, so she put Eddie and me to bed, told us not to get up until she got back, and went looking for Jimmy.

Soup led the way to where Jimmy sat dazed in the snow, bleeding from a gash on his head. While he was chopping wood, he had swung the axe up and back, and the heavy iron head had flown off and knocked him down. Rose struggled to get him to his feet and half carried, half led him back to the house. She made Eddie and me get dressed, put on our coats, and bundled us in quilts into the backseat of the car. She managed to get Jimmy in the car, also quilt wrapped, and she drove all night, about three hundred miles, to Okreek, where Eddie and I were left with Grandma Harriet.

Grandpa Ed went on with Rose to Mission, where they made a brief stop to pick up the Driving Hawks, then drove on to the Rosebud hospital, where Jimmy was diagnosed as having a severe concussion.

Rose shivered and shook her head as she recalled the incident. "I've never been so scared. It was so cold—the car heater didn't begin to keep us warm. I prayed the whole way that the old car wouldn't break down. I guess I could have taken Jimmy to the doctor in Bonesteel, but I wanted to get home."

Rose had no family or close friends in Milk's Camp to go to for help. She was lonely at Ponca Creek, although I didn't know it then. Jimmy was often away at his WPA jobs or responding to a middle-of-the-night summons because of the illness or death of some member of his congregation. When word came about Rose's sister Alma's tragic death as the result of an exploding stove, I vividly remember Rose weeping with deep wrenching sobs as she sat on the steps of our little house with only Eddie and me trying to comfort her. "Don't cry, Mama," we urged, patting and hugging her. We didn't understand how she could weep so, and we were frightened to see her distress.

But most of my memories of Ponca Creek are happy ones. I was innocently unaware of our poverty; I don't recalled ever being hungry or cold.

I remember going with Mother to the ladies' extension classes at the Milk's Camp Day School, where a white female agent showed the women how to prepare the commodity foods issued to the Indians during the depression. Once, I was happily stuffed with grapefruit, part of the commodity ration that the congregation didn't like and gave to us.

Our life was centered around church activities and the day school, which was also the Milk's Camp community center. Periodically, we went there to get commodities issued from the school warehouse. In the summer we'd help weed and hoe the large community garden planted on the school grounds. Dad helped with the harvest; then we'd stay at home with him while Mom helped process the vegetables in the cannery. She'd come home with a box of canned corn, green beans, and other vegetables—our part of the produce, which each family shared.

Community meetings were held at the school, which also served as the polling place for the newly enfranchised Indians. The whole community came to see the children perform in the Christmas program, and Jimmy went there once a week to give religious education before such instruction was banned. This was where, when only five, I started the first grade and learned to read. Reading came easily to me, and I came to love words, which let my mind soar into a universe I had never known was there. Mr. Miller, my first teacher, was delighted and encouraged by my fledgling flights with books from his personal library.

Sundays, of course, the people came to church. Mother played the organ, making sure that Eddie and I were seated on the front pew by the organ, where she could keep an eye on us. I stayed put, enjoying the music and singing Lakota even though I didn't understand the words. However, as soon as Mother started pumping the organ and her hands were busy on the keys, Eddie escaped, crawling under the pews, over kneelers and people's feet—all the way to the rear and out the door.

Winyan Omniciye, the women's guild, met in the members' homes, but other gatherings were held in our house, which had one large kitchen–living room and one small bedroom. Some nights I'd fall asleep to the close harmonic tones of "Skeeters am a humming on the honey suckle vine . . ." of the Milk's Camp barbershop quartet, who practiced at our house. Asampi, Chief Milk, was dead then, but his grandson sang baritone to my father's tenor.

Sometimes during the night, I'd awaken to radio music and my parents' laughter as they danced to big band sounds. The battery-powered radio brought drama and humor into our home with Fibber McGee, the Lone Ranger, Ma Perkins, and other radio plays, to which I created pictures in my mind. But we liked the music best.

Dad had learned to play the trombone in school, and I'd tease him to play for me; sometimes he would, but not too often because some member of the congregation was always dropping in. Music was important to him; in fact, he played trombone with the reservation dance band, Chief Crazy Horse and the Syncopators, "but I'm not enjoying it, so much, so I guess those days are over for me," he wrote in 1936.

After we moved to Okreek, I took piano lessons and felt so grown up accompanying Dad's trombone improvisations—until his lips got sore. Then he'd shake his head, wipe his mouth, and put the horn away. Mrs. Red Buffalo was shocked when she came into the house unannounced to find Jimmy teaching me to dance to music from the radio.

After I learned to play the organ, some Sundays Dad would take me with him to the reservation chapels that he served. My legs were barely long enough for my feet to pump the pedals, but I began being a church organist. I also began learning to drive on those Sundays in the fall so that Dad could hunt pheasant on the way to and from the chapels.

James's diaries are daily recordings of his pastoral duties, with rare notations of a personal item. In June 1942, he made a brief mention of our trip to the Black Hills with stops at Wind Cave, Iron Mountain, Mount Rushmore, and Rapid City. My memory of that trip is not of the Black Hills but of an incident en route that I later included in an essay, "Special Places" (1978).

Travel during wartime was a hazardous adventure on old patched tires and gas rationing. It was hot, and our old Chevy had a canvas water bag tied to the front of the radiator in case the car overheated and for drinking when we got thirsty. I had a stomachache in anticipation of the adventures ahead.

We had been holding our breath for miles, praying that the few drops of gasoline left in the tank would get us to the next town and a gas station. I had to go to the toilet again. Dad complained at the frequency of my need, which called for many stops and a run for the ditch. So I was doubly glad to see the gas station and hoped for the privacy of a privy and maybe even running water.

While the car was at the pump, I ran to the back of the station and saw three doors: MEN, WOMEN, INDIANS. WOMEN was locked, so I rushed into INDIANS, trying not to breathe the foul air or sit on the soiled stool.

As we resumed the journey, I thought about the three doors. "That gas station had three rest rooms," I told my parents. "One for men, one for women, and one for Indians."

I remember Mom and Dad looking at each other as I went on, "Isn't it nice that there was a special place for Indians?"

No one said anything for a while; then Dad patted my knee. "My girl, I hope there will always be special places for you."

Years later, when I was aware of the bigotry and prejudice that existed outside my secure family, I remembered Dad's words. I learned that I had to create my own "special places" because no one else would provide them.

Okreek was a special place for me. I was pleased that the house we lived in had an upstairs with one side that I could call "my room." I could be by myself to read and dream. It wasn't much more than an attic, but it became the garret of Louisa Mae Alcott's little women and Dickens's London.

I remember Christmases in Okreek, although I wished we could have our own Christmas tree. There was one tall tree in the guild hall, but it was for the whole congregation. On Christmas Eve old and young gathered in the hall for a meal and gifts. The tree was trimmed with handkerchiefs, which were gifts for the men and women. Every child got an apple, an orange, and a paper bag full of candy, and as the excited young ones clutched the fruit and dug into the candy, loud stomps and a deep bass "Ho, ho, ho!" were heard at the door.

"Sh, sh," the adults commanded. "Listen! What's that?"

Round-eyed children crept close to mothers as the door opened and with a gust of cold air Santa Claus came in. Some children screamed with fright, never in their life ever seeing such a figure, all in red, with a bushy white beard. But Santa calmed them with soothing Lakota and gave each child a ball, top, car, or doll.

Then we all walked up the hill to Calvary Church for the midnight service. It was a mystical place at night, with swags of greenery and lots of candles, for there were no electric lights. Carols, sung in Lakota, rang through the night, but I rarely managed to stay awake for the whole service. At its end, we'd stumble down through snow to a cold house and beds, for we'd never leave a fire in the wood stove when no one was there.

The next morning Grandma and Grandpa Ross joined us, Robert and Flora Driving Hawk having come the night before, and we opened our family gifts before Jimmy had to drive off to the chapel at Ideal for the Christmas service there.

Some of our gifts were clothing that came in the Mission boxes sent from wealthy Episcopal churches in New England. It was an exciting time when the boxes came, for I helped unpack. Often I'd find a glamorous ball gown with "jewels" or one of slinky velvet. Sometimes there were shiny worn dress coats with funny tails and white bibs and black bow ties. The adults would laugh at the impracticality of such articles of clothing, but when Mother let me wear them, it was fun to play dress up and become a debutante.

Mission box time was also disappointing because we never got first pick of the practical dresses, underwear, trousers, shirts, shoes, and coats. "The people need them, more than we do," Mom gently explained.

One fall I had grown so tall so fast that my winter coat was too small. I prayed for a just-my-size coat to come in a mission box—the same place I'd gotten my present coat the year before, only then the sleeves hung over my fingers, leaving growing room. Now, the hemline came above my knees, my wrists stuck out like skinny sticks, and the coat was tight over my shoulders.

The boxes came, and there was the most beautiful coat I had ever seen. It was a smooth, grayish, soft fur. "Ooh," I tried it on, enthralled with its sleek warmth. It was perfect—only a little long, and I could wrap it around me twice. But with all my heart I wanted that coat. Of course, I couldn't have it, but every day I came home from school and checked to see whether it was still hanging in the rummage room. Then it was gone, and I was heartbroken.

The next day, it was cold and rainy. I miserably donned my old coat, tied on a scarf, and pulled on mittens, but there were four inches of bare skin between mitten and sleeve. It was a bitter walk to school. I took my coat to the cloakroom, and there, hanging on the first hook, was the fur coat. It wasn't until school was out that I found out who had claimed the fur. It was a cold, wet walk in the rain. All the

Episcopal kids were going to the guild hall for the weekly youth meeting, and Pauline Wright walked beside me in the fur coat.

"I'm so glad I got this *new* coat," she said. (I thought she gloated.) "It's so warm and keeps me dry. Aren't you cold?"

Miserably I nodded my head, but said nothing about her *new fur coat*. But I saw out of the corner of my eye that it almost dragged on the ground and that its hem was wet and splashed with mud.

In the guild hall we stood near the wood stove to warm ourselves before the meeting. Soon a dank aroma filled the room as our damp coats steamed and dried. "Phew," one of the boys said. "Pauline, your coat smells like a wet dog," and everyone laughed.

I was glad that I wasn't wearing that coat, and Pauline, embarrassed by the "wet dog" remark, never wore it again.

That time in Okreek was during World War II, and along with other men whose grandfathers had been Sioux warriors, James enlisted in the U.S. Army. But he failed the induction physical because of a stomach ulcer. In 1944, he was given permission from the bishop to enlist in the marines, but he was once again disappointed when his stomach problems kept him a civilian.

The next summer Rose and Jimmy went to find work in Sioux Falls, South Dakota, leaving Eddie and me with our Ross grandparents. Rose recalled the few weeks in the city.

"We went together, hoping to find work in the same place. The Cataract hotel needed maids and dishwashers." My fair-skinned mother was hired immediately, but there was no job for my near full-blood father. The only place that would hire Indians was the slaughter room at Morrell's Packing Plant.

> Jimmy would come home reeking, and he couldn't eat even after he bathed—he could still smell the stuff. It was a bad place and made him sick. But we needed the money, so we stayed.
>
> I'd go to work at the hotel. The maids were not to be in the rooms if the guests were there. I knocked at the door of this one room, no one answered, so I went in. I started my chores, then all of a sudden there was this man there—without any clothes on. I ran out of the hotel. We came home the next day.

In 1946, Dad had surgery to remove a cancerous stomach tumor. He had to undergo surgery again in 1947, but the cancer spread, and he died in the Yankton hospital on 22 May 1948.

My father remains young in my memory; he died when he was

thirty-four and I was fourteen. But in those brief years his values permanently affected my life. He carried me on his back to school during a snowstorm because it was important that I not miss a day of my education. He insisted that I learn English well because of the hard time he had in school knowing only Lakota. He helped me learn to read the hard stories from *The Book of Knowledge,* and his Christian faith inspired mine.

My father's decision to become a priest of the Episcopal Church was the result of his parents' devout Christianity, which began with the conversion of Pejuta Okawin, Lucy High Bear. He also respected and admired the dedication of Hannah and Charles Frazier, whose strong faith allowed them to survive personal tragedy while they ministered to the Indians. They and other Indians who first converted to Christianity lived their religion in a way few whites of the same time period did and few whites or Indians do today.

The raising up of Indian people to minister to their own race served the evangelical nature of Christianity, but it also provided education and employment to the Indian men and women who answered the call.

Pejuta Okawin, who was baptized Lucy and married James Clairmont, resided at Ring Thunder's camp on the Rosebud reservation not far from where Charles and Hannah Frazier were stationed at Salt Camp. After the Dawes Act of 1887, which permitted the allotment of 160 acres per adult and sixty acres per child, Ring Thunder and his band received land along the Little White River. The camp was the site of St. John's Episcopal Station, a small framed church and mission building built in 1884.

There was a close kinship between the Clairmonts and the Ring Thunders in *tiyospeye* (extended family). All their allotted land was in the same area on the Little White River, and their community was named Ring Thunder. Over one hundred years after Ring Thunder was established, my brother, Edward Driving Hawk, was given the name Can Gleska Wakinyan by relatives in the same community.

Lucy Clairmont and Hannah Frazier were contemporaries on the Rosebud, but unlike Hannah, Lucy spoke only Lakota and never went to school. Both exemplified the lifestyles of Indians on the early reservations. As the missionary Elaine Goodale Eastman recalled, there were "two distinct worlds existing side by side, now in dramatic opposition, now intimately mixed. There were already a few Dakotas at home in the white man's world. There were also a good many of both races who belonged as much to one as to the other" (see Graber 1978, 33).

By 1891, the Rosebud people were living in log houses in their *tiyospeyes* (extended family villages). Elaine Goodale described such a community:

> The people live in scattering villages of fairly comfortable log cabins, surrounded by small farms, and use their tents only in hot weather and on their frequent journeys to and from the Agency for rations. These little hamlets are often very prettily situated on the banks of a winding stream fringed with a low growth of timber. . . . A modest frame chapel, surmounted by a cross and bell-tower, frequently adorns some little eminence near the center of the village. (Eastman 1891, 1)

Lucy's family had adopted white-style clothing, not because they wanted to, but because they no longer had access to the game that had fed and clothed them in the past. The men wore woven trousers and shirts and favored the black reservation hat, yet they still preferred moccasins to hard shoes. Lucy wore leggings on which she had worked a quill design, and her moccasins were either quilled or beaded, but her ankle-length gown was of calico, not leather.

Lucy High Bear Clairmont was an active member of the St. John's congregation, and she had no more difficulty living this new religion than she had the old. She attended the 1897 Niobrara Convocation of the Episcopal Church when it was held at St. Mary's School on the Rosebud. The Episcopal Church began its work among the Sioux with the Santees, an outreach that was officially titled the "Missionary Jurisdiction of Niobrara" but that encompassed work among all the Sioux tribes. Its first convocation was held at Santee in 1870, but later convocations alternated among the different reservations every year.

Although no Indian ceremonials were incorporated into either this gathering of the Indian Episcopalians or the annual mission meetings of the Presbyterian Church, such meetings served the same social function as the old Sun Dance, when friends and relatives from all directions came together in the summer. Christian Indians from different reservations camping together was not unlike the traditional camp circles in which the Brulé, Minneconjou, and other tribes had their own, allotted places.

Lucy was among the first generation of Indian women not to have known the independent prereservation life, but her role, as wife and mother, was the same as her mother's, Skanskanwin's, had been when religion was an integral element of daily life. While learning Christian tenets from the white women missionaries, Lucy learned to make clothing out of cotton, using a sewing machine with a steel needle and cotton thread to stitch the garments together, thus replacing skins laced with sinew. Her fingers used to porcupine quillwork now learned to bead, crochet, embroider, and quilt.

From the missionary women, Lucy also learned to cook new foods on an iron stove in her log cabin at the same time as she heard the gospel. It was not that difficult for her and other Indian women to adapt to this new life, for they were still wives and mothers, and they adapted traditional customs to the new religion.

Indian women became the steadying center of the family. The male warrior-hunter, however, lived a life without purpose on the reservation. He was a relic of a once-glorious past, and he frequently turned to alcohol to ease his distress. Many women supported their families financially by selling their quill-, bead-, and leather craft work and then their star quilts. The quilts, utilitarian in purpose to replace buffalo robes and wool blankets, gave color to the drab decor of the log cabin and ultimately became an art form among Sioux women.

The women of Lucy's and, later, Flora's congregations formed a close bond because of this sharing in times of sorrow, but also because their formal group, Winyan Omniciye, was a vital part of their community's life. Even though they now lived separately on individual allotments, the custom of women working together prevailed despite the distance between families. In addition to coming together to quilt, they shared their work in community gardens and gathered to pick wild plums, choke cherries, and other berries; they helped each other process the fruit by drying it or making *wojape* (cherry pudding) and jellies. They also worked together to pick, husk, and dry corn.

As a child, I helped my grandmothers dry corn in a manner similar to the Santee method described earlier. After picking and husking ripe ears, Harriet Ross parboiled the corn before shelling it with a sharpened spoon. Flora Driving Hawk eliminated the boiling but shelled it the same way. The corn was then strewn in a thin layer on a wire screen, which was placed in the sun and covered with a muslin sheet to keep the flies out of the sweet, milky mass. The drying process took several days, and my duty was to pick the wee green bugs out of the finally dried corn. The dried kernels were stored in tin cans and cached under beds. Later, during the 1930s, when communal gardens in Indian communities such as the one at Milk's Camp were popular, all the families who helped sow, weed, and water the crops and harvest and process the produce in the community cannery also shared in the final product. Grandmother Harriet and my mother learned to use smaller pressure canners in their homes in order safely to process vegetables and meat in jars for family consumption. Canned venison and corn is delicious, but the elderly preferred the dried because, as Flora said, "It don't taste as good from a can."

Today, I don't can vegetables because of the easy availability of groceries in supermarkets, but I do dry corn for the occasional treat of dried corn soup for family gatherings. The first time I did it, I followed the same method my grandmothers used up to the drying part. I remembered the tedious chore of removing bugs, so I put the wet corn in panty hose, which I then hung on the clothesline to dry. Not only did this look strange, but the kernels stuck to the nylon, making it difficult to remove the corn, and the bugs got in anyway. Offended by the sight of droopy, bulging panty hose and bugs in his soup, my husband built a dehydrator to speed up the process and keep out all the bugs.

The purpose of reservation women working together remained the same as in the prereservation era: to share their labor, to teach the young, and to chaperone young girls. On the reservation, grandmothers and mothers couldn't as easily serve as chaperones, but they kept a strict eye on the girls (as mine did me)—to keep them pure as the White Buffalo Calf Woman had directed.

My grandmothers, Harriet and Flora, often visited each other, and I used to sit near them as they recalled with nostalgic humor how strict their mothers, aunts, and grandmothers had been. "They watched us all the time. We couldn't be alone with a boy for one minute. We [girls] always had to go together so we wouldn't get in trouble." (I experienced similar chaperonage and concern in the 1950s.) They also recalled the instruction they received at the time of their first menstrual flow, noting that a woman didn't talk about such things when men were around.

"It wasn't like it used to be. We didn't have to go off by ourselves until we stopped bleeding, but we had to keep our bodies clean and our thoughts pure. We were told that we were women now; we could have babies, but not until after we had a husband."

The instructions my grandmothers received were not given in the formal Buffalo Ceremony, but it was of the same nature, and those instructions were in turn instilled in my mother and me.

Instructions to a Girl Becoming a Woman
(from the Buffalo Ceremony, a retelling)

The spider is an industrious woman.
She builds a tepee for her children
and feeds them well.
The turtle is a wise woman.
She hears many things
and saves them for her children.
Her skin is a shield,
An arrow cannot wound her.
The lark is a cheerful woman.
She brings pleasant weather
to her lodge.
She does not scold.
She is always happy.

In those early reservation days, a girl was still encouraged to respect her brother, and the first pair of moccasins she made was for him. Flora Driving Hawk recalled that she had made a pair for her brother, "but they didn't fit, and he threw them in the creek." When asked if his rejection of her gift had made her angry, Flora replied, "No, I had to learn to make better ones."

A girl could do kind things for her brother that did not require speaking directly to him or staying too long at his side. In a study of kinship patterns among the Lakota (Pine Ridge), Vernon Malan called this the "primary avoidance pattern," which served as a model for correct adult behavior (see Malan 1958).

Such avoidance also prevented incest, although Malan did not come right out and say so. Perhaps the right questions were not asked, or perhaps the people he interviewed were reluctant to discuss such a heinous act. Such topics and other intimate subjects, either of a sexual nature, including menstruation, as noted earlier, or concerning bodily functions, were not discussed in mixed company. My Rosebud grandmothers *oh heenhed* over a woman who was a devout Christian but had to her shame borne a child to her brother.

This act was abhorrent because a brother was supposed to protect his sister from the unwelcome attentions of young men and later from abusive husbands.

Flora and Harriet spoke of a woman they knew who, even though now a practicing Christian, still followed the traditional mourning ritual. "She cut off her hair, and her legs were all cut up, and blood was running down to the ground as she walked to the cemetery."

Neither of their mothers, Hannah Frazier or Lucy Clairmont, would have mourned this way because of their total acceptance of Christianity. But Skanskanwin and Hazzodowin would have expressed their grief by pulling out their hair or hacking it off with a knife. They might have slashed their arms, legs, and breasts and wailed and wept continually until after the loved one was buried. Neither did Flora or Harriet mourn in this manner, but they sympathized with women who still did.

At the death of her last child, my father, Flora Driving Hawk covered her head and wept with deep, wrenching sobs, her tears soaking her shawl. At James's funeral, her women friends, her Lakota "sisters," wailed and keened in a heartrending tremolo amid a torrent of tears. Today at funerals this still happens, with not only family but also friends and acquaintances sharing grief by embracing the mourners and weeping with them. In so doing they physically empathize with the mourners as well as mourning past losses of their own again. Contemporary non-Indians who repress their sorrow and bear their grief stoically are overwhelmed by the Indians' emotional expressions of shared grief; they often have to struggle to control their tears, which seem to flow contagiously in these outpourings of group sorrow.

It was in this way that Harriet and Flora mourned the death of a lifetime friend, Elizabeth Red Buffalo, whose sudden death seemed so unnecessary to me. Harriet had been summoned by the family to care for her friend's body before the undertaker arrived. Harriet, shocked to find Elizabeth's eyes still open, placed coins on the lids to hold them shut, and put a roll of toilet paper under the chin as if the proud woman were still holding it up, and bathed her friend's stiffening corpse. Even in death, the woman must be presentable.

Elizabeth had been the only woman passenger in an automobile full of men, and even though her husband and son were among them, she could not bring herself to tell them of her need to relieve herself, so her bladder ruptured, and she died in the car.

Flora and Harriet shook their heads over their friend's needless death. "She shouldn't have been so 'bashful,' " my grandmothers said of their friend's modest reserve, but they respected her for it even in their grief at her death. Elizabeth had done what a woman was supposed to do: be modest, not going around calling attention to herself.

My grandmothers were also modest women, never expecting recognition for their accomplishments, and uncomfortable if they received any. Harriet made dolls, tedious, slow work, all done by hand, even the bodies, which were hidden under the small leather garments. But when Mrs. Barbour, the wife of an Episcopal priest, said, "Your dolls are beautiful," Harriet merely nodded and put them away. For many long years, Harriet was the organist for her church, but when, in front of the whole congregation, the priest lauded Harriet's devotion and skill, she kept her eyes lowered and barely nodded in acknowledgment. My mother played the same organ, and years later so did I, but when the priest noted that I was following a tradition, and everyone in the congregation was looking at me, I was so embarrassed by this attention that I kept my eyes on the organ keys.

To this day, I am uncomfortable with being publicly recognized for my accomplishments. If recognition was given to a woman, it was given to her whole family, so it was important that she conduct herself so as never to bring shame on herself and thereby on her family. I have received an invaluable legacy from the diverse cultural elements of my family, and this has been the theme of my work. Were it not for the support of my family, I would never have tried to publish what I had written.

In my youth, an Indian girl's destiny was to be a wife and mother, but a few still sought visions and became medicine women. Flora Driving Hawk's mother, Pejuta Okawin, was a medicine woman, but to Flora's knowledge she did not receive her healing gifts from a vision. Nor did Flora know whether her mother engaged in other shamanistic works as did the Rosebud medicine woman my grandmothers talked about, who may have been the one described in an incident at Parmalee on the Rosebud around the turn of the century:

> There was a g-r-e-a-t big thunderstorm coming up. A man on a horse (a haranguer) went down the line. "Get ready! Be careful!" he shouted. . . . My mother said, "This storm is coming

after one of the Indians. They had a dream about this thunder . . . the thunder warned them that if they don't sacrifice a dog the lightning is going to strike somebody."

. . . but the medicine man wasn't a man at all—he was a woman!

She had a whole bunch of sage braided—made like a crown and she wore it on her head. Her dress was all ripped up! At the hem it was like a fringe.

She was standing out by herself. The rest of the Indians were dressed in costume, singing and dancing around that pot of dog soup. The dog soup was boiling so fast it was just white and that old lady stuck her hand into the pot and brought out the dog's head. (Lewis 1980, 254)

Lucy treated many ills, but she had no cure for the tubercle bacillus that infected and killed her. Her grandson, James, had an active case, which might have meant placement in the dreaded Sioux Sanatorium in Rapid City. But "Father Barbour wouldn't let him go," Flora recalled, "because everyone who went there died."

Father Barbour recommended exercise, and for months, every day, James ran at least two miles from Mission to the Rosebud Boarding School, and healed himself.

Pejuta Okawin died in 1904, drowning in her own blood. Tuberculosis wrought havoc among a people who in the past moved their home when its site was soiled. The confining closeness of a one-room log house was ideal for breeding disease. Indian families had once rolled up the bottom of the tepee to allow fresh air to circulate. But Indian homemakers were ignorant of the necessity of cleaning a house that couldn't be moved. It wasn't until after Flora returned from boarding school to watch over her young brothers and care for her sick mother that Lucy's log home was cleaned.

Flora had attended St. Mary's Episcopal School for Indian girls. Originally established in 1874 at Santee as an industrial school for girls, St. Mary's was destroyed by fire in 1884 and rebuilt on the Rosebud in 1885. The academic program included reading, writing, arithmetic, and geography, but the greatest emphasis was on domestic skills. Elaine Goodale Eastman described how this skill improved a girl's home: "Such a house as this a typical Indian cabin of the poorest sort—will be made a hundred times more attractive within by the deft fingers of the little daughter who has learned to wash dishes, sweep, and make neat beds at the school" (1891, 201).

Flora and other St. Mary's girls were proud of their training, and so was Bishop Hare (founder of the school), who reported, "One can pick out a St. Mary's girl where ever she goes in the Indian country by the kind of home she keeps" (1977b, 102).

Even though as an adult Flora was proud of being a St. Mary's girl, she had not been the willing student that Harriet Frazier had been at Santee. "I went to school when I was seven years old. The first thing I remember is the noise. Clompity clomp clomp clompity—it sounded like lots of woodpeckers at a hollow tree."

Flora remembered that a white woman hurried to the door, "clompity clompity clompity"; her long dark skirt swirled about her ankles, revealing the black shoes on her feet. Flora looked at the feet of the other white woman and realized that the "clompity" noise was the clatter of stiff, hard-soled shoes on the wood floor.

"I'll never forget that first night," Flora recalled. "They lined us all up. Made us take off our clothes, and put kerosene on our heads to kill the bugs. They washed us. Took us upstairs and put us to bed and turned out the lights. There was no one to say good night to me. I was so lonesome—I cried all night."

In addition to learning basic domestic and academic skills at St. Mary's, all the girls learned to play the organ so that they could be organists in their home churches. Organ lessons remained part of the St. Mary's curriculum when the school was again moved, this time to Springfield, South Dakota, across the river from its first home at Santee. It was at Springfield that I was a St. Mary's girl in the 1940s.

After her mother's, Lucy's, death, Flora's father married twenty-one-year-old Lizzie "Winnie" Steed, only four years older than Flora. Flora then attended the Indian school at Chamberlain, South Dakota, where she met Robert Driving Hawk.

Robert Driving Hawk was born about 1885 on the Lower Brulé Reservation, Dakota Territory, and knew very little of his family history. His father's name, Chanshkan nah ho pah, was translated and written as "Driving Hawk" by Lower Brulé Agency officials, with his first name listed as "Jacob." Robert did not know how his father got his name, but he did know that Chanshkan nah ho pah had two wives. The first wife, noted as "Mrs. Driving Hawk" on a Bureau of Indian Affairs determination of heirs, but to whom Robert referred as "Ina," was the mother of Robert and Virginia, my namesake; the second wife was the mother of Henry, Joe, and Annie Driving Hawk.

Ina (the name means "Mother") died when Robert was a child, and he had no recollection of her. He was raised by the second wife.

I remember Robert as a tall, quiet man who listened while Flora talked. My time was spent with my grandmothers and other female relatives, and Robert adhered to that tradition. I have a faint memory of sitting in his lap and laughing as he tickled my neck with his few chin whiskers. Another time I had an excruciating earache, and again he held me and blew warm, soothing smoke into my ear. During one of the summers my brother and I spent with Robert and Flora, he took us fishing, baited my hook for me, and, after I happily caught one, took the fish off. I learned to go to him whenever Flora reprimanded me because he'd tell her in firm Lakota to leave me alone.

Some sixty years later, in my home, Flora recalled her courtship and marriage.

> They expelled him [Robert] because they caught us standing in my blanket one night. We weren't doing anything bad, and there were others out there too. He went back to Lower Brulé and built a house on his allotment. He didn't say anything about getting married.
>
> I went home to my father's, but didn't like it too much. But then Robert came after me.
>
> It was cold, but he hitched rides with the mail from Lower Brulé to Rosebud. Then he walked to Ring Thunder to get me. He wanted to take me to Lower Brulé to get married, but I was afraid he couldn't when we got there, so we got married at Rosebud. My dad didn't want me to, but I did.
>
> We rode the mail wagon to Valentine [Nebraska] and got on a train to Sioux City [Iowa]. There were some Oglalas from Pine Ridge on the train who were going overseas. They were going to dance over there with some cowboy and Indians doings. One of them was my aunt, who got upset when she saw me with Robert.
>
> "Are you running away with this man?"
>
> "No, we're married," and I showed her the license to prove it.
>
> She was happy for me. She gave us a chunk of *wasna* that she broke off of a big piece that she was taking overseas in case there wasn't anything to eat over there.
>
> It was evening when we got to Sioux City. It was the biggest place I'd ever seen, and I was scared. Robert found us a hotel

room. I was so scared, I made him sit on a chair in front of the door—all night.

Long years after Robert's death, as Flora told this story, she wept and said, "Poor thing. I made him sit up all night, and it was his wedding night."

The next morning the couple boarded another train to Chamberlain. When they reached the Missouri River town, Robert's uncle was waiting with a team and wagon to take them to Lower Brulé, which was across the Missouri from Crow Creek, which had become a Yanktonai reservation after the Santee had left. "I don't know how he knew we were coming," Flora recalled, "but he was there.

"Right after we got there, I made Robert take me to the Episcopal Church, so that the priest [the Reverend Luke Walker] could bless us."

The newlyweds moved into the house that Robert had built for the bride he went to Rosebud to get. But Flora, so homesick that she cried all the time, persuaded Robert to take her back to Ring Thunder.

While Flora was away, her father had tried to claim her land, but "the agent wouldn't let him." James Clairmont apparently accepted this decision and helped Robert built the house where David, Paul, Margaret, Elizabeth, Virginia, and James were born. Only James, my father, lived to adulthood.

Flora held her hand over her eyes and wept, sadly reliving the deaths of her children. Paul and Elizabeth died as infants; four-year-old David died on 19 April 1920 and two-year-old Margaret on 5 May of the same year, both victims of the influenza epidemic that swept through the Rosebud.

"I don't know how they got it," Flora wondered some sixty years later. "I kept them clean and didn't let them run around the agency like some of them [the other Indian mothers] did." She wept more as she told how a year later, on 5 July 1921, eleven-year-old Virginia died of diphtheria in Robert's arms.

In 1925, Flora and Robert moved to Mission town, where he operated the Phillips 66 gas station. While in Mission they served as custodians of the Trinity Episcopal Church. Flora was a member of Trinity's Winyan Omniciye for thirty years. In 1943, Flora and Robert moved to Springfield, South Dakota, the third site of St. Mary's School, which had moved from Mission in 1923. There they worked as janitor and laundress until 1953, when they retired to Mission and resumed their service to Trinity Church. Robert died in 1957, Flora in 1977.

After Robert's death, Flora lived by herself in the two-room house, originally built for James and his bride, Rose. Her half-brothers, David and Dick Clairmont, visited her frequently, and there were many women of her age in Mission who called her "sister" in the Lakota fashion. She was "auntie" to other adults—Indian and non-Indian—and "grandma" to the children. To former St. Mary's girls, who dropped by whenever they passed through Mission, she was "Mrs. DH." But her treasured relatives were her grandchildren, who no longer lived on the reservation. We saw her briefly on annual summer visits.

The small house had electricity, but Flora hauled her water from the well; she used the privy in the summer and a slop pail in the winter. "When I get my Black Hills money, I'm going to get a bathroom," she used to say, referring to the claim the Sioux wanted from the government for the illegal taking of the Dakota mountains in violation of the 1868 treaty.

Her meals were cooked on a kerosene range. A wood-burning stove adequately heated the two rooms, and her brothers hauled in a wood supply every fall.

Fiercely independent, she held to her ways, and when her grandson Edward gave her an oil burner, she gave it away to someone who needed it. I gave her my inherited share of the land settlement after the Corps of Engineers damned the Missouri River, flooding Robert's Lower Brulé allotment. I urged her to buy a refrigerator, but she used the money to have a memorial giveaway for Robert. I couldn't attend the memorial, which was held in the Calvary Church guild hall at Okreek on Ascension Day, 15 May 1958. Over one hundred people were present, and Flora made sure everyone received a gift. The major gifts of star quilts were presented to the clergy and the men who had been pallbearers at Robert's funeral.

In the summer of 1968, she tripped on the steps to the house and broke her foot. The fracture was slow to heal, and she became dependent on a walker and a cane to move about. Afraid of falling again, she was overly cautious, and her leg muscles atrophied, which further frightened her. She managed well enough, but when winter came, I took her to live in my home in Flandreau, South Dakota.

My husband and I were teachers at the Flandreau Indian School, and our children were in school, so Grandma was alone on week-days. She could not help with the housework or cooking, which frustrated and saddened her. "I might as well die," she'd complain. "I'm old and useless."

She was homesick and missed her Lakota "sisters." Her eyes were still sharp and her fingers nimble enough to thread a needle, so we went to town and bought material for her to make a star quilt top.

She had made many of these quilts in her lifetime, and she used her cardboard diamond template painstakingly to cut the hundreds of pieces needed for the quilt. Her design was the traditional "Sioux star"—one large, eight-pointed star pieced from the multicolored diamonds on a white background.

She was patient in her work. The diamond pieces, cut on the bias, had to be individually stitched together in the right way so that the star would not be crooked. She scornfully told of women who hurried their quilts so that the tops bunched and would never lay flat. She sewed on the quilt from September until the end of March, when she went home. The next year she again stayed the winter and made a second quilt top. Both quilt tops were for my two oldest children, and when the youngest was born in August 1970, her eyesight had become so poor that she could no longer see to make her tiny stitches. She felt badly about this and apologized for having to buy one for him.

Every day, Grandma sat by the window in her room after the family had left the house. Her failing eyesight needed the best light as she stitched quilt pieces together; it was also a good spot to watch the activities of the neighborhood, which she reported to me at the end of each day.

It was a quiet neighborhood, with little traffic and few passersby, but Grandma came to know its habits.

She knew the time of day without looking at the clock. First, an elderly couple walked by each morning on their way to seven o'clock Mass at the Catholic church, heading home forty minutes later. Every day, about eight thirty, the man down the street either walked or drove his pickup downtown. The lady across the street, the hem of her white uniform showing below her coat, left for the clinic at ten to nine.

Vance and I came home for an hour's lunch break. The mailman came around two. The children were home from school by four and Vance and I by five fifteen.

Grandma knew what day of the week it was by what regularly happened in the neighborhood. On Monday, about nine, the milkman delivered to the lady next door and the garbage truck rattled down the alley at ten. Tuesdays, a man in bib overalls delivered eggs across the street. An elderly woman walked by every Wednesday afternoon with a shopping bag on her arm. Each Thursday, the senior citizen's van honked, and the lady next door ran to board it.

Nothing regular happened on Friday.

During the Indian Summer days of October, Grandma watched the neighbors raking leaves, taking in geraniums, digging gladiola bulbs, and covering roses.

In the early false spring that came in February, the neighbors were out again, impatiently testing the garden soil to see whether the frost was out. They chatted and laughed while they hung laundry to dry in the damp breeze. Grandma laughed too and predicted a blizzard.

But it was the cold, snowy days that were drearily monotonous for Grandma. There was only falling snow to watch and howling winds to hear. Then she huddled over the heat vent by her window, glad that she didn't have to haul wood for her stove.

After each fresh snowfall, the neighbors were out shoveling and chatting with each other, if it wasn't too cold. They were nice people in our neighborhood, many elderly widows, like Grandma, but they were white people. They knew she lived in my home and saw her peering out at their daily activities. Once in a while, one would wave to her, but no one ever visited her.

Grandma had company only once in the three winters she lived with us, when two Indian women visited for an afternoon. She spoke about that visit many times after; they'd promised to come again, but never did.

She didn't go to church with us because its steps were too steep and she was afraid of falling. My husband was the lay reader, and I the organist, and a visiting priest came once a month; Grandma was grateful when he brought Communion to her.

The days, the months, the winter passed slowly for Grandma. She never complained of being lonely, but she did sulk on occasions when we unintentionally slighted her. My husband teased her about her weather predictions. In the dry Rosebud country, foggy days were rare in the winter, but they occurred frequently in the Flandreau area along the Big Sioux River. The first time she awoke to the dense, white mist so thick she couldn't see across the street, she warned, "There's going to be a bad snowstorm."

But days passed, and no storm came, just the usual spate of snow. On another of several foggy days, my husband teased, "Think we're going to have a blizzard, Grandma?"

"Hmph," she said, and for the next several days addressed him only in Lakota, refusing to speak English to him.

We never did get the bad storm that she predicted, but she told me that she had been born in a blizzard in a tent, which led me to write

> Tble,
> Named for the cold star
> appearing after the blizzard
> ceased its wail.
> Hers filled the tent
> at life's first shock.
> Birth wet, Tble,
> Steaming in the frigid air.

She was called Ebbly, short for Emily (her middle name), at home, but her Lakota name was Telewi, which she said was "Morning Star." Her younger brother mixed the two names and called her "Tble."

One morning she was waiting for me as I came downstairs. She was agitated and nervous. "Did you hear the owl last night?"

I hadn't, but she insisted that she had. "Someone's going to die," she said.

I tried to calm her, but for the next several days she worried about our health, insisting I call my brother to see whether his family were all right. Weeks passed, and I had forgotten about the ominous warning the owl had brought, when she met me at the door when I got home from work. "Here," she thrust a letter into my hand. It was from a Mission friend of hers who wrote of the death of one of Grandma's Lakota sisters.

Grandma sat with us in the evenings and on weekends, enjoying our company. She loved to listen to her great-grandchildren's chatter and laughed when they did. She frequently asked me to play the organ, requesting her favorites from the Lakota hymnal. Sometimes she sang with me.

One noon, I came home to find her sitting on the floor of her room sewing on the quilt. "It's getting heavy," she explained as I helped her to her feet.

As the star pattern of the quilt grew larger, it was difficult for Grandma to hold its bulk as she sewed, and we placed another chair by the window to hold the quilt.

She hummed or whistled her beloved hymns as she worked; sometimes she smiled and chuckled to herself, remembering a happy episode from the past. Or she would pause in her sewing to wipe away tears before they fell on the quilt.

When I had time to sit with her, Grandma told me stories. Not the ones I knew as a child, but family tales, which were vivid in her memory.

The last winter she was with me was after my brother and his family had moved back to the Rosebud and she had been living with them at the "home" place near Ring Thunder. Ed was running for tribal chairman, and he worried about Flora, now in a wheelchair, often alone with two grandsons. Tribal politics are often "no holds barred" affairs, and after an opponent's supporter had physically threatened Flora and the boys, I took Flora back to Flandreau.

This time she worried about Ed and his family, fearing "something bad was going to happen." I tried to reassure her, but would often awaken at night to hear her talking loudly—sometimes in English and then in Lakota—with long pauses as if she were responding to someone's questions.

"Who were you talking to, Grandma?"

"The old man," which is what she used to call Robert. "He and my children come sit on my bed at night."

I was alarmed, even though she seemed rational and the nightly conversations seemed to calm her. I called the doctor, who explained that because of her low blood pressure, her circulation was poor and her brain wasn't getting enough oxygen. What she saw in her mind was very real to her. He prescribed medication, which helped, but now I worried because I knew of the belief that dead relatives visited the living to take them "home." If the time was right, the person went with them.

It wasn't the right time for Flora, who lived eight more years, but she insisted on going home to Ring Thunder. Before she left, she reminded me to get the "wedding tops" quilted, then urged, "You learn how so that you can make quilts for your grandchildren."

BIBLIOGRAPHY

Anderson, Clayton, and Alan R. Woolworth, eds. *Through Dakota Eyes: Narrative Accounts of the Minnesota War of 1862.* St. Paul: Minnesota Historical Society Press, 1988.

Anderson, Harry H. "Fur Traders as Fathers: The Origins of the Mixed-Blooded Community among the Rosebud Sioux." *South Dakota Historical Society Quarterly* (Pierre) 3, no. 3 (Summer 1973): 233–70.

Armstrong, Moses K. *The Early Empire Builders of the Great West.* St. Paul: E. W. Porter, 1901.

"Big Missouri Winter Count." St. Francis SD: Buechel Memorial Lakota Museum, 1973.

Bordeaux, W. J. *Conquering the Mighty Sioux.* Sioux Falls SD: 1929.

Brevet's South Dakota Historical Markers. Sioux Falls SD: Brevet Press, 1974.

Brown, Joseph Epes. *The Sacred Pipe.* Baltimore: Penguin Books, 1971.

Chittenden, Hiram M., and Alfred T. Richardson. *Life, Letters, and Travels of Father Pierre Jean DeSmet, S.J.* Vol. 2, *1801–1873.* New York: Francis P. Harper, 1905.

Deloria, Ella Cara. *Dakota Texts* (1931). Edited by Agnes Picotte and Paul Pavich. Vermillion SD: Dakota Press, 1978.

——. *Speaking of Indians.* New York: Friendship Press, 1988a.

——. *Waterlily.* Lincoln: University of Nebraska Press, 1988b.

DeSmet, Father Pierre. "Register" (copy). St. Francis SD: St. Francis Indian Mission, n.d. (covers 1849–74).

Driving Hawk, Flora Clairmont. Conversations. Flandreau SD, 1968–72.

Driving Hawk, James H. Diaries, 1936–47. Rapid City SD.

Driving Hawk, Virginia. "My Family History." Undergraduate term paper, South Dakota State College, Fall 1952. (Based on interviews with Hannah Howe Frazier and Harriet Frazier Ross.)

Eastman, Charles A. *An Indian Boyhood.* New York: McClure Co., 1907a.

——. *Old Indian Days.* New York: McClure Co., 1907b.

Eastman, Elaine Goodale. "The Indian Girls in Indian Schools." *Home-Maker* (June 1891): 199–205.

Episcopal Mission Records. "Book A" (covering Rosebud Mission, Santee Mission). Sioux Falls SD: Archives of the Episcopal Diocese of South Dakota, Center for Western Studies, 1874–88.

Folwell, William Watts. *A History of Minnesota.* Vols. 1, 2, 3, 5. St. Paul: Minnesota Historical Society, 1921.

Frazier, Rev. Charles. Journal, 1931. Edited and translated by Art Raymond. Grand Forks ND.

Gilkerson, Peggy. "Missionary Rivalries among the Santee Sioux." M.A. thesis, Department of History, Harvard University, 31 March 1961.

Graber, Kay, ed. *Sister to the Sioux: The Memoirs of Elaine Goodale Eastman, 1855–91.* Lincoln: University of Nebraska Press, 1978.

Hafen, LeRoy R. *The Mountain Men and the Fur Trade of the Far West.* Vols. 1–10. Glendale CA: Arthur Clark Co., 1968.

Hafen, LeRoy R., and Francis Marion Young. *Fort Laramie and the Pageant of the West, 1834–1890.* Glendale CA: Arthur H. Clark Co., 1938.

Hare, Rt. Rev. William Hobart. *Annual Reports of the Missionary Bishop of Niobrara.* New York: Bible House, 1873–93.

Hassrick, Royal B. *The Sioux: Life and Customs of a Warrior Society.* Norman: University of Oklahoma Press, 1964.

Heard, Isaac V. D. *History of the Sioux War and Massacres of 1862 and 1863.* New York: Harper & Bros., 1863.

Hickerson, Harold. *Sioux Indians.* Vol. 1, *Mdewakanton Band of Sioux Indians.* New York: Garland Publishing Co., 1974.

Hughes, Thomas. *Indian Chiefs of Southern Minnesota.* Minneapolis: Ross & Haines, 1969.

Hyde, George E. *Spotted Tail's Folk: A History of the Brule Sioux.* Norman: University of Oklahoma Press, 1961.

Irving, Washington. *Astoria.* New York: George P. Putnam, 1851.

Jackson, Donald, ed. *The Journals of Zebulon Montgomery Pike.* Vols. 1, 2. Norman: University of Oklahoma Press, 1966.

Jackson, Helen Hunt. *Ramona.* Boston: Little, Brown, 1900.

———. *A Century of Dishonor: The Early Crusade for Indian Reform.* Edited by Andrew F. Rolle. Reprint. Gloucester MA: Peter Smith.

Jones, Blossom Steele. Interview. Rapid City SD, 20 September 1985.

Keating, William H. *Narrative of an Expedition to the Source of St. Peter's River, Lake Winnepeek, Lake of the Woods . . . Performed in the Year 1823 by Order of the Hon. J. C. Calhoun, Secretary of War, under the Command of Stephen H. Long.* 2 vols. Philadelphia: H. C. Carey & I. Lea, 1824.

Kingsbury, George W. *History of Dakota Territory.* Vol. 1. Chicago: S. J. Clarke Publishing Co., 1915.

LaPointe, Mary H. Ross. Interview. Rapid City SD, 8 July 1990.

Legends of the Mighty Sioux. Pierre: Workers of the South Dakota Writers' Project Works Projects Administration, 1941.

Lewis, Emily H. *Wo'wakita: Reservation Recollections.* Sioux Falls SD: Center for Western Studies, 1980.

Linderman, Frank B. *Red Mother.* New York: John Day Co., 1932.

McFarling, Lloyd. *Exploring the Northern Plains, 1804–1876.* Caldwell ID: Caxton Printers, 1955.

Malan, Vernon D. *The Dakota Indian Family.* Bulletin no. 470. Brookings SD: Rural Sociology Department, South Dakota State College, May 1958.

Marken, Jack W., and Herbert T. Hoover. *Bibliography of the Sioux.* Metuchen NJ: Scarecrow Press, 1980.

Marryat, Frederick. "Captain Marryat in Minnesota, 1838." *Minnesota History* 6 (1925): 168–84.

———. "An Upper Mississippi Excursion of 1845." *Minnesota History* 22 (March 1941): 29–30.

Meyer, Roy W. *History of the Santee Sioux.* Lincoln: University of Nebraska Press, 1967.

Moorehead, Warren. "Sioux Women at Home." *Illustrated American,* 31 January 1891.

Neill, Edward D. *History of Minnesota.* Philadelphia: J. B. Lippincott & Co., 1858.

O'Meara, Walter. *Daughters of the Country: The Women of the Fur Traders and Mountain Men.* New York: Harcourt, Brace & World, 1968.

Paulson, T. Emogene, and Lloyd R. Moses. *Who's Who among the Sioux.* Vermillion SD: Institute of Indian Studies, University of South Dakota, 1988.

Poole, D. C. *Among the Sioux of Dakota: Eighteen Months Experience as an Indian Agent* (1881). Reprint. St. Paul: Minnesota Historical Society Press, 1988.

Posey, Rose Ross. Interview. Rochford SD, 15 June 1986.

———. Interview. Rapid City SD, 14 August 1991.

Powers, Marla N. *Oglala Women.* Chicago: University of Chicago Press, 1986.

Rencountre, Estella Frazier. Interview. Rapid City SD, 12 July 1989.

Riggs, Mary B. *Early Days at Santee.* Santee NE: Santee Normal Training School Press, 1928.

Riggs, Stephen R. *Tah-Koo Wah-Kan; or, The Gospel among the Dakotas.* Boston: Congregational Sabbath-School and Publishing Co., 1869.

———. *Mary and I: Forty Years with the Sioux.* Chicago: W. G. Holmes, 1880.

Riley, Glenda. *Women and Indians on the Frontier, 1825–1915.* Albuquerque: University of New Mexico Press, 1984.

Robinson, Doane. *A History of the Dakota or Sioux Indians*. Pierre: South Dakota State Historical Society, 1904.

———. "Sioux Calendar." In *Encyclopedia of South Dakota*. Pierre SD: Doane Robinson, 1925.

Ross, Donald D. "Maiden's Leap." In *Forgotten Heritage*. Winnebago NE: Nebraska Indian Press/Nebraska Inter-tribal Development Corp., 1978.

Ross, Donald D. Telephone interview. Rapid City SD, 10 December 1990.

———. Interview. Rapid City SD, 8 October 1991.

———. "The Frazier/Ross Family Tree." Wait Hill NE, n.d.

Sandoz, Mari. *These Were the Sioux*. New York: Dell Publishing Co., 1967.

Saum, Lewis O. *The Fur Trader and the Indian*. Seattle: University of Washington Press, 1965.

Schoolcraft, Henry Rowe. *Narrative Journal of Travels through the Northwestern Regions of the United States, Extending from Detroit through the Great Chain of American Lakes, to the Sources of the Mississippi River . . . in the Year 1820* (1821). Reprint. New York: Arno Press, 1970.

Seymour, Flora Warren. *The Story of the Redman*. London and New York: Longmans, Green, 1929.

Shea, John D. G. *History of the Catholic Missions among the Tribes of the United States, 1529–1854*. New York: P. J. Kennedy, 1854.

Sibley, Henry H. *Iron Face: The Adventures of Jack Frazier, Frontier Warrior, Scout, and Hunter*. Chicago: Caxton Club, 1950.

Skinner, Alanson. *Anthropological Papers of the American Museum of Natural History*. New York: American Museum of Natural History, 1915.

Sneve, Virginia Driving Hawk. *Betrayed*. New York: Holiday House, 1972a.

———. *High Elk's Treasure*. New York: Holiday House, 1972b.

———. *Jimmy Yellow Hawk*. New York: Holiday House, 1972c.

———. *The Chichi HooHoo Bogeyman*. New York: Holiday House, 1975a.

———. *They Led a Nation*. Sioux Falls SD: Brevet, 1975b.

———. "Grandpa Was a Cowboy and an Indian." In *Images*. New York: Scott Foresman, 1977a. Private reprint, 1982. Reprint, Pierre SD: Dakota West, April 1985.

———. *That They May Have Life: The Episcopal Church in South Dakota*. New York: Seabury, 1977b.

———. "Special Places." In *The Ethnic American Woman*, ed. Edith Blicksilver. Dubuque IA: Kendall/Hunt, 1978.

———. "Story Tellers." *Plainswoman* (Grand Forks ND) 8, no. 1 (September 1984).

Standing Bear, Luther. *My People, the Sioux*. Boston: Houghton Mifflin Co., 1931.

Tabeau, Pierre-Antoine. *Tabeau's Narrative of Loisel's Expedition to the*

Upper Missouri (1939). Reprint. Norman: University of Oklahoma Press, 1968.

Tibbles, Thomas H. *The Ponca Chiefs*. Lincoln: University of Nebraska Press, 1972.

Tripp County South Dakota: 1909–1984 Diamond Jubilee. Freeman SD: Tripp Co. Diamond Jubilee Committee, 1984.

U.S. Department of the Census. *Dakota Territory, 1880*. Microfilm rolls 111, 113. Washington DC, 1880.

U.S. Department of the Interior. Bureau of Indian Affairs. Rosebud Agency Allotment Records. Rosebud SD, n.d. (covers allotment period 1889–1934).

———. Rosebud Agency File. Aberdeen SD: Aberdeen Area Office, n.d. (covers 1874–1920).

———. Santee Agency File. Aberdeen SD: Aberdeen Area Office, n.d. (covers 1868–90).

Vestal, Stanley. *Sitting Bull, Champion of the Sioux*. Boston: Houghton Mifflin Co., 1932.

Weist, Katherine M. "Plains Indian Women: An Assessment." In *Anthropology on the Great Plains*, ed. Raymond Wood and Margot Liberty. Lincoln: University of Nebraska Press, 1980.

Welsh, William. *Sioux and Ponca Indian Reports*. Philadelphia: M'Calla & Stavely Printers, 1870.

———. *A Month among the Indian Missions*. New York: American Church Press, 1872.

Wilder, Laura Ingalls. *Little House on the Prairie*. Reprint. New York: Harper & Row, 1971.

Young Bear, Myrna. "Spider's Winter Count." In *Papers of the 18th Dakota History Conference*. Madison SD: Dakota State College, 1987.

Zitkala-Sà. *Old Indian Legends*. Boston: Ginn and Co., 1901.

WINNERS OF THE
NORTH AMERICAN INDIAN PROSE AWARD

Boarding School Seasons: American Indian Families, 1900–1940
Brenda J. Child

Claiming Breath
Diane Glancy

*They Called It Prairie Light:
The Story of Chilocco Indian School*
K. Tsianina Lomawaima

Son of Two Bloods
Vincent L. Mendoza

All My Sins Are Relatives
William S. Penn

Completing the Circle
Virginia Driving Hawk Sneve

Printed in the United States
36325LVS00006B/49-96

9 780803 292543